North Cascades National Park Service Complex

Ebey's Landing National Historical Reserve

Museum Management Planning Team

Jonathan Bayless, Park Curator
Golden Gate National Recreation Area
San Francisco, California
Team Leader

Robert Applegate, Archivist
Nez Perce National Historical Park
Spalding, Idaho

Kelly Cahill, Park Curator
North Cascades National Park Service Complex
Marblemount, Washington

Kirstie Haertel, Archeologist
Pacific West Region
Seattle, Washington

Diane Nicholson, Special Projects Curator
Golden Gate National Recreation Area
San Francisco, California

Department of the Interior
National Park Service
Pacific West Region
2005

North Cascades
National Park Service Complex

Ebey's Landing National Historical Reserve

Museum Management Plan
January 2005

Recommended by:

_____

Kent Bush, Lead Curator
Pacific West Region

Concurred by:

_____

William Paleck, Superintendent
North Cascades National Park Service Complex

_____

Gretchen Luxenberg, Superintendent
Ebey's Landing National Historical Reserve

Approved by:

_____

Jon Jarvis, Regional Director
Pacific West Region

Executive Summary

The Museum Management Plan for North Cascades National Park Service Complex (NOCA) and Ebey's Landing National Historical Reserve (EBLA) identifies the museum management issues facing the parks, and presents recommendations to address them. A team of museum management professionals developed this plan in full cooperation with the staff responsible for managing park archives, museum collections, and library resources.

The museum and archival collections of the two parks differ in size and complexity. North Cascades collections have been developed over many decades and contain diverse subjects and material types. Ebey's Landing's collections are quite new and concentrate on archeological excavations. The construction and expansion of the Marblemount museum facility gives North Cascades an important role in regional and network museum operations, serving not only Ebey's Landing, but also San Juan Island National Historical Park. As the complexity and amount of work continue to grow, the museum program will require increased levels of support and resources to meet the challenges it faces.

North Cascades and Ebey's Landing have many outstanding opportunities for the growth and use of object and archive collections to support their mission and serve the public. Further progress requires management support at the highest levels. This plan calls for a number of actions that are intended to remove obstacles that have stymied the effective management of museum resources for many years. It also brings together additional expertise to address some of the museum issues that have suffered from unintended consequences of past approaches.

This Museum Management Plan recommends actions designed to take the park archives and museum resources through a developmental phase that will provide for the documentation, preservation, and management of these park-specific resources.

Key Recommendations

Key recommendations are listed here while more detailed action recommendations follow each issue section of the plan:

- Conduct an archival survey and assessment for all park records.

- Bring together archeologists and curators to address the potential research use and culling of archeological collections and protocols for new collecting.

- Complete construction of the Golden West Lodge at Stehekin storage room and develop Standard Operating Procedures (SOP) for access.

- Begin planning and compliance for a new addition to the Marblemount curatorial facility.

- Develop methods to document the acquisition process of new collections.

- Dedicate time and effort to de-accession inappropriate collections.

- Explore ways to treat the Buckner Homestead and Historic District as a cultural landscape and manage the historic items outside the context of the museum program.

- Seek additional funding and positions to fully staff the museum program. Make the NOCA curator position full-time, and add network museum technician and archivist positions.

Table of Contents

List of Illustrations

Tables

The Museum Management Plan (MMP) replaces the Collection Management Plan (CMP) referred to in the National Park Service publications, *Outline for Planning Requirements,* DO#28: *Cultural Resources Management,* and the *NPS Museum Handbook,* Part I.

The CMP process generally concentrated on the technical aspects of museum operations. As a holistic approach to museum management planning, the MMP evaluates all aspects of museum-related programs within a park, and makes broad recommendations to guide development of park-specific programs that address the park's identified needs within the context of a five-year implementation plan.

The MMP recognizes that specific directions for the technical aspects of archival and collection management exist within the *NPS Museum Handbook* series. It does not, therefore, duplicate that information. Instead the MMP places museum operations within the context of park operations by focusing on how various collections may be used by park staff to support the goals of these particular parks. This plan recognizes that there are many different ways in which archives and museum collections may be organized, linked and used within individual parks, so it provides park-specific advice on how this may be accomplished. Where required, technical recommendations not covered in the *NPS Museum Handbook* will appear as appendices in this plan.

The plan was completed as a team effort with many discussions with park staff, although the issues were written by individual team members. The authors by issue are:

Issue A: Robert Applegate
Issue B: Kirstie Haertel

Issue C & D: Jonathan Bayless
Issue E & F: Diane Nicholson

The planning team wishes to thank the staff of NOCA and EBLA for their cooperative and many efforts to make our visit both productive and enjoyable. The plan could not have been accomplished without their dedication and devotion to the mission of the National Park Service.

North Cascades National Park (NOCA) was created in 1968 to preserve the rugged beauty of the North Cascades Mountains and their jagged peaks, deep valleys, cascading waterfalls, and over 700 glaciers. North Cascades National Park Service Complex contains the heart of this mountainous region in three park units which are all managed as one and include North Cascades National Park, and Ross Lake and Lake Chelan national recreation areas. Each area contains wilderness and offers different experiences.

1968 – 1982

From 1968, when the North Cascades National Park Service Complex was established, until the early 1980s, the museum collection was managed by NOCA's Division of Interpretation, and collection items were retained at three sites, Marblemount, Sedro Woolley, and Stehekin. A collateral duty position under the Division of Interpretation covered work in museum management.

A herbarium was created at headquarters in Sedro Woolley through the efforts of volunteer botanists Ralph and Dorothy Naas. They began collecting and mounting specimens and by 1983, when formal collection accessioning and cataloging began, the park herbarium contained approximately 5,000 specimens. Other natural history objects, such as vertebrate study skins and skeletons, wet specimens and geological specimens, were also collected during this period. They were prepared by park personnel and were gradually added to the collection. By the 1980s, a small assortment of historical artifacts had also been collected from various sites. A photograph collection was established with field collections from U.S. Forest Service files at Marblemount Ranger Station, with transfers from nearby Forest Service Ranger Districts, and with donations from private citizens. Unfortunately, many of these early collections lacked any documentation of the original source or history.

Prior to 1977, when NOCA headquarters moved to a new location in Sedro Woolley, active management of the collection was minimal. Items were stored in boxes and a few museum cabinets, which were housed in the lab or the interpretive specialist's office. The herbarium received the most attention. After the move, the collection was consolidated into a dedicated space. Without professional curatorial oversight, however, this room became disorganized storage for non-museum materials as well.

At the Skagit District Ranger Station in Marblemount, a collection of historical artifacts was assembled. They were stored in a variety of substandard locations, ranging from the interpreter's office for photographs to an outdoor area known as the "bone yard" for mining and logging-related artifacts assembled from field sites. This material was not accessioned or cataloged.

Historical objects comprised the Stehekin District collection. In the 1970s NOCA acquired lands in the valley that contained large numbers of potential museum objects left by the former landowners. What became known as the Weaver collection consisted of abandoned historic (mostly household) artifacts collected by park personnel from the Weaver home site on Weaver Point. The material was stored in boxes on the floor of the top story of the deteriorating Golden West Lodge. In 1976 a history professor from Pacific Lutheran University and a NOCA seasonal interpreter found and studied some Weaver family correspondence. The professor processed the material and developed a finding aid for it. Some of the material later suffered water damage from a leak in the Golden West Lodge roof.

Another purchase was the Buckner Homestead property including a house, outbuildings, and an assortment of historic artifacts related to Buckner family life and the operation of the orchard throughout the first half of the 20th century. Ownership of the artifacts was unclear for many years after the NPS acquired the land. In 1974 a long-term agreement between Harry Buckner and NOCA was reached regarding fourteen of the larger, more significant objects such as tractors, sprayers, and wagons. The rest of the material remained undefined. When Mr. Buckner died a couple of years later, ownership of the material came into question again. Negotiations with the Buckner family continued for the next twelve years. Throughout this period, NOCA did not designate the material as museum property because of the lack of clear title. Although NOCA considered the site an interpretive exhibit, the objects were not cared for or preserved; most of it was outdoors in the environment.

The first archeological collections were generated under contract as part of the North Cascades Survey from 1977-1979, and from site testing at Newhalem for the visitor center construction project in 1989.

1983 - 1993

A turning point for collection management at NOCA occurred in 1983. Through efforts of the chief naturalist and the Pacific Northwest regional curator, work was started on a Scope of Collection Statement (SOCS) and a Collection Management Plan (CMP). The SOCS was drafted and finally approved in 1984. The CMP was contracted and written in 1984-85. It was never finally approved, although it was used as a working document for several years. The draft CMP proposed that three separate and independent collections be retained at NOCA. Headquarters in Sedro Woolley would hold the herbarium and natural history objects; Marblemount District office would hold historical collections pertinent to the west slope; and the Stehekin District Office would have its own pertinent cultural resource and natural history collections. This proposal was only partially implemented. Until the late 1990s, the Stehekin District collection remained independent from NOCA's other museum collections. In 1988 the Resource Management Division took over management of the collections.

Formal accession and catalog documentation began at NOCA headquarters in 1983. Most of these records were lost, and the objects were later re-cataloged. From 1985 to 1987 volunteers and temporary staff cataloged a large part of the herbarium, resulting in about 5,000 records. During this period the Automated National Catalog System (ANCS+) was introduced at NOCA. From 1988 through 1990, seasonal museum technicians were hired with Backlog Cataloging funds to complete cataloging of the herbarium, study skins, and wet specimens. In 1989 a major effort was initiated to reorganize and complete many old accessions. NOCA began monitoring environmental conditions with a hygrothermograph in the collections room in 1983. NOCA headquarters moved again in 1988, with collections moving to a warehouse where the climate was partially controlled, and conditions highly variable. Museum cabinets were acquired for all headquarters objects. All interleaving newspaper was removed from the herbarium in 1991. The preservatives of many wet specimens were changed from formaldehyde or Wardol to ethanol or Wardsafe by 1994.

From 1988 to 1991 archeological survey and testing work by Archeologist Bob Mierendorf in the Ross Lake NRA produced many artifacts, which were housed in a remodeled room in the Ranger Warehouse in Marblemount. The artifacts were placed on shelves or in museum cabinets, and a hygrothermograph recorded that the room had few environmental controls. Funding for cataloging archeological collections was provided by the Seattle City Light and the Skagit Environmental Endowment Commission as part of the dam re-licensing mitigation. Housing the large number of artifacts (40,000) and herbarium specimens prompted management to look at the needs of museum collection storage.

In 1990 funding was authorized for a new museum collection storage facility with environmental controls. NOCA acquired additional funding to enhance the facility with curatorial and cultural resource offices and work space. Collections and staff moved into the Marblemount Curation Facility (MCF) in 1994. Environmentally controlled and secure collection storage space totaled 600+ square feet.

1994-1998 — Changes in Collection Management

In 1992 a Collection Management Plan was written, and approved in 1994, to assist park management in administering the development of the museum collection, and to provide specific actions to improve the collection over a five-year period. A term museum management technician was hired to prepare for the CMP and to manage the museum collection to NPS standards. In support of the 1994 CMP, the park in 1995 created the Cultural Resources Branch within the Resource Management Division. Two Pacific Northwest Region employees duty-assigned to NOCA were transferred to the park organization and became the Cultural Resource Branch chief and park archeologist. At this time, responsibility for museum management moved into the Cultural Resource Branch, and the museum technician position was established as a permanent, subject-to-furlough, upward-mobility journeyman position. This effort to professionalize and upgrade the museum technician to a museum curator position was accomplished by 2002.

Historic photographs and maps were acquired from diverse sources—former park and forest service staff, area residents, children of notable figures, and park supporters.

The Buckner loan agreement of 1988 consisted of 50 objects. The rest of the material at the Buckner Homestead was deeded to NOCA as a gift. The Buckner collection continued to deteriorate in historic buildings and on the grounds. The Buckner Homestead Historic Landscape Plan and management documents were created in 1995 to serve as guidance. Recommended actions for museum collections have yet to be implemented. An object inventory was taken in 2003, and comparative conditions of these items were documented photographically.

The transfer of San Juan Island NHP historic archeology collection from the University of Idaho to the Marblemount Curation Facility occurred in 1995. The artifacts were unpacked and organized in the NOCA collections drawers and cabinets until there was no room left. The remaining artifacts were stored in Buckhorn boxes on top of cabinets.

Collection Condition Surveys were completed in 1998 for NOCA by Diana Dicus and for SAJH in 1998 by Tamsen Fuller. The surveys provided needed baseline inventories of condition assessments, but little conservation work has resulted.

1998-2002 — Multiple Park Management Begins

The museum computer systems were continually evolving, as were the back-up media. The ANCS+ database was upgraded to a Microsoft Windows interface and images could be attached to records. The data conversion was fraught with difficulty, and quirks in the software still raise questions of data fidelity and quality assurance. The natural history species names can not be parsed into the format of the program. At this time about 10,000 specimens needed their scientific names updated. As the collections have been moved several times within the storage area since 1998, the location information also changed. A substantial amount of staff time will be needed to complete these updates, and to make the ANCS+ database fully functional.

For several years, the curator-of-record for SAJH invested the majority of time, dollars, and effort on the SAJH prehistory archeology collection. Agreements were entered into, University of Washington facility conditions were surveyed, artifact inventory was attempted at the Burke, and the Burke database for ANCS+ was lost. During this time of fiscal belt-tightening, the recurrent theme of non-NPS institutions charging to house NPS museum collections arose nationwide. The SAJH prehistoric archeology collection at the Burke Museum Archeology Department at University of Washington was subject to the fee-storage review.

While touring the Burke collection, the curator documented non-secure and substandard facility conditions at the UW Burke Museum Archeology Department and Archeology Department storage located in Kane Hall. Environmental deficiencies and overcrowding of artifacts were observed in both building basements. Upon negotiation between the NPS and the Burke Museum, prehistoric artifacts for study remained at the Burke Museum; security and storage of NAGPRA–related artifacts were improved; and the Kane Hall sediment samples were moved to the SAJH collection at NOCA.

With the acceptance of bulk sediment samples from UW, more storage room was needed. Cabinets and cabinet tops in Marblemount Curation Facility storage were overcrowded and items spilled into the halls. With

Museum Collection Protection and Preservation funds, construction began on an adjoining 960 square foot collection storage room at the Marblemount Curation Facility. Unfortunately, a lack of locational data or a storage plan compounded the overcrowding and the accountability deficiencies.

The Tabor Geology Collection was accessioned and partially cataloged by a geology student in 2002. The researcher/donor provided excellent documentation, and the collection is accompanied by a geology tour book, "Geology of the North Cascades."

The 1996 collection of aquatic insects by park ecologist Reed Glesne added depth to the park faunal list. The insects were cataloged in 2001, and stored in a newly renovated Seattle City Light building in Newhalem dedicated to NPS collection storage and laboratory activities.

Archives were accessioned and finding aids created for records acquired in the mid-1990s. A call for additional archival materials went out in 2002. The NOCA Administrative History generated eight linear feet of archives which support the assertions and footnotes in this document. A finding aid was started in 2003, and is under development.

2002-2004 — Collection Development and Access

In 2002 museum staff began moving SAJH collections to the dedicated SAJH addition at the Marblemount Curation Facility. The first wave of moved objects included the sediment samples from UW Kane Hall. Some historic artifacts and archives were also placed in the SAJH room. The herbarium was filled in 2003 by the 2002 SAJH forays conducted by NOCA botanists. In 2004 the SAJH superintendent and chief of resource management toured the facility, and then assisted in moving the majority of historic artifacts from the NOCA room to the SAJH room. The effort is ongoing, with the curator conducting a 100% in-house inventory of every catalog number encountered, noting condition and documenting the storage location.

Historic building stabilization compliance work at Ebey's Landing National Historical Reserve, which began in 2001, produced the beginnings of an archeology collection for the reserve. The collection was on loan and housed at NOCA. A formal Letter of Agreement between NOCA and EBLA was signed in 2004 transferring collection management to the NOCA curator. Archeological artifacts were cataloged at NOCA and a team led by the Fort Vancouver NHS archeologist assessed and described the EBLA collection in 2004. The accession is 75% cataloged. A Scope of Collection Statement has been drafted.

Both of the above activities affected NOCA collection management. Moving SAJH artifacts into the SAJH storage space freed NOCA collections storage in the NOCA room for NOCA objects. Storage floor plans and storage plans for both rooms were deemed imperative prior to further moving, unpacking, and storage.

As part of the Natural Resource Challenge, the North Coast and Cascades Research Learning Network was established in 2002. Inventory and Monitoring Program (I&M) baseline data is continually being added to the NPSpecies database. Research permits result in collections, reports, and associated materials, but the tracking of the progress and disposition of these collections and reports has been incomplete and fragmented. Interactions with the I&M program data manager and science advisor are limited by time and coordination factors. A system for follow-up on research permit collections and reporting activities needs to be addressed nationally, with NOCA leading the fray in examples of need.

Herbarium collections by UW research forays and baseline inventories increased the herbarium collection by another 2,000 specimens; additional herbarium cabinets will be added in the near future. Contracts to survey plant communities created baseline information for planning and mitigation in rock climbing areas and road clearing excavation. Also, the first collections in the park of lichens, liverworts, and mosses were documented by Martin Hutten in 2004.

The Misch Geology Collection was accessioned in 2003. It is the first and most complete story of geologic processes and their results in the North

Cascades region. Dr. Peter Misch, who taught generations of Washington geologists from 1948 to 1990 at the University of Washington, held theories and facilitated tests which supported the major tenets of plate tectonics. His 3,000 hand specimens, thin sections, and field notes were in need of a home with the UW geology building undergoing renovation. Since site localities in the park are so well documented, the park is fortunate to be the repository of this collection. It is in need of cataloging, but the field notes are in the UW Natural Resource Archives. Archival access through duplication will directly assist in the catalog effort.

The Buckner Homestead Historic District continues to be managed as a historic cultural landscape, with few farming elements surviving to preserve. The NOCA employees living on site have protected the basic existence of farm machinery, but the condition of farm materials slowly degrades. An inventory of plants and cultural scatter would document a snapshot in time, but the involvement of curators at the site has been minimal.

Digital data format is of increasing concern in collections management. A survey of backup tapes, floppy disks, and CDs and their readers was recently undertaken. An upward migration of data was completed, and computer systems are being upgraded. Obsolete media and readers have been disposed of by the NOCA Property Officer. Acquisition of digital scanners and their application has created the potential for sharing archives, artifact and object information, and images. Since scanning is labor intensive, numerous volunteers have been utilized to digitize documents, transcripts, and images. Collecting digital information from researchers offers an additional means of searching information. Storage of digital media and the incumbent responsibility of its migration to current media also need attention.

The Marblemount Curatorial Facility provides a setting for researchers, educators, and park staff to come together to share knowledge and expertise, and to discuss current research in meetings, seminars, and classes.

Ebey's Landing National Historical Reserve Collections

Ebey's Landing National Historical Reserve (EBLA) is a National Register historic district that was established by Congress as a unit of the National Park system in 1978 to preserve and protect a rural community that exhibits Pacific Northwest history in its place names, archeological sites, historic buildings and structures, and historical land use patterns. It is a nationally significant cultural landscape that represents a continuum of humans interacting with their environment from prehistoric times to the present. It is approximately 17,400 acres in size, and about 90% of the land is privately owned. The NPS has no authority over local government.

EBLA is managed by a unit of local government, as required by the enabling legislation. This unit of government was defined with the creation of the Trust Board of Ebey's Landing NHR, a mostly volunteer board of citizens who live in the area and are appointed by the four governmental entities that represent EBLA: town of Coupeville, Island County, Washington State Parks, and the National Park Service. The trust board does not have authority over any of these government partners. The role of the board is to serve as the umbrella organization that works to ensure the reserve moves into the future with its character and integrity intact, all within the context of a working, living, and viable modern community. The National Park Service allocation for EBLA in FY2004 was $209,500. Approximately half of that amount goes to the trust board as a matching grant for its operations. Both NPS and the trust board have limited staffing capabilities.

Background of Collections at EBLA

The legislation establishing the reserve never intended the NPS to be a large landowner within EBLA. The NPS role is to provide technical assistance in matters of land protection, historic preservation, and interpretation. Establishing museum collections were not a part of the trust board's mission, nor the NPS vision or mission for the Reserve. The Island County Historical Society and Museum have been the "keepers" of Island County history, including the area within which the reserve is located. The trust board did create a slide library to document the reserve landscape and to facilitate giving interpretive programs. Photographs and maps have also been collected for resource management, land protection, and interpretive work. In the Resources Management Plan, written and approved in 1995 and updated in 1999, a project statement addressing collections was developed ("Prepare Scope of Collections Statement"). This statement was the extent of the attention paid to collections, as additions to the collection were not anticipated at the time.

Since the creation of EBLA, a number of events have occurred which have caused increasing concern about collections management needs. The NPS and trust board embarked on an ambitious oral history program in the 1990s which resulted in dozens of taped interviews, transcripts, reproductions of photographs. and other ephemera. After 25 years of existence, the trust board and NPS have created administrative files and records for the unit. An administrative history was prepared in 1993, and records accumulated for that research study were retained. Also, after the NPS received the historic Ferry House from The Nature Conservancy as a donation, stabilization work immediately began on this significant structure. The preservation work on the foundation resulted in artifacts and samples being uncovered and collected. At the same time, the historic Jacob Ebey Blockhouse was being rehabilitated by the NPS, and again, artifacts were collected from that foundation work.

Present and Future Collections Management Needs

EBLA now has artifacts that need cleaning, cataloging, and culling by experts. The reserve has a draft Scope of Collections statement in place which needs final approval. There is no staff for collections management work at EBLA. The reserve relies solely on the North Cascades National Park Service Complex's curator who, under signed agreement, serves as the curator-of-record for EBLA. Each year EBLA makes an attempt to provide funding to offset NOCA staff time, and in 2004, $1600 was given to NOCA as reimbursement. EBLA has no storage capabilities for museum collections, so NOCA is serving as the repository for the artifacts. Additional collections management work will need to be done at EBLA, for many other historic structures owned by the NPS will require compliance activities and rehabilitation work. This will likely result in more artifacts being added to the collection for documentation, review, and study. Funding for an archives project has been requested.

A general management plan is currently underway at EBLA and the needs of the archives and collections are being addressed in the plan. One alternative calls for the possibility of having the local museum serve, in part, as a repository of some Ferry House and other artifacts, in order to keep these valuable assets in a local setting. However, the local museum is currently not able to provide that space and service, resulting in NOCA remaining the primary facility for EBLA collections. As a result EBLA will continue to require space and staff time from NOCA to meet the ever-growing demand for data management and reporting necessary to meet NPS requirements.

Collections Philosophy

The basic principles for managing museum collections in national parks are not always well understood. Park managers, resource managers, and interpreters are often too busy with their specialties and daily work to fully consider the concepts and logistics governing collection management. It is easy for parks to fall short of developing a sound museum management program and, as a result, not realize the full benefit and value from their collections.

This section provides the following background information about museum collections:

- The purpose of museum collections
- How museum collections represent a park's resources
- Determining where to locate museum collections
- Establishing access, use, and management policies for museum collections

Purpose of Museum Collections within National Parks

Museum collections contain objects and specimens, and most museums administer their own archives and operate their own libraries. These functions are necessary to support the work of the organization as a whole. It is not unusual for these resources—archives, collections, and libraries—to also be accessible to the public.

Within national parks, museum collections (including archives) serve four basic functions:

- **Documentation of resources** - Park collections should serve as documentation of the physical resources of the park as well as the history of the park's efforts to preserve and protect those resources.

- **Physical preservation and protection of resources** - Park collections should help preserve and protect a park's resources, not only by keeping the specimens and collections made to document the resources, but also by preserving information about the individual items and the resource as a whole. This is central to the management of both natural and cultural material.

- **Research** - During documentation of collections, a park performs research to provide the background information used in cataloging. The park is also responsible for making this collections information available to legitimate research, which can itself lead to new discoveries about an individual item, or the park as a whole.

- **Public programs** - The park is responsible for using its collections to provide information to the public. Exhibits and publications are two traditional means of supplying public programs, but new technology has led to other communication methods, including electronic access through web sites and online databases.

How Collections Represent a Park's Resources

A park's museum, library, and archival collections provide different perspectives on its resources:

Museum collections, which contain three-dimensional objects and specimens, should represent the resources within the park boundaries. Examples of museum collections include: artifacts from archeological compliance activities; specimens and resulting reports from resource management projects; and paint samples and building fragments from restoration of historic structures.

The park archives may contain files, manuscripts, maps, building plans, and photos that document the history of park development and the management of its resources. Individual collections within the archives should further document the activities that created portions of the museum collections. Examples of park archives include: copies of field journals and maps created while collecting botanical specimens; photographs taken during historic structure work; maps and as-built drawings made during utility installation; and property, land, and water use agreements that document past acquisition and use of park lands.

The park library contains both published literature and less formal reports and documents relevant to the park's resources and their management. Examples might include: general literature concerning local history, flora and fauna; specialized scientific studies involving biota and archeological resources found in the park; circulating copies of park specific planning documents; trade, craft and professional journals reflecting the need for park staff to remain current in their field.

Determining Where to Locate Park Collections

The *NPS Museum Handbook* should be used as a guideline for identifying locations for branch or satellite park collections, and establishing methodologies for their documentation, organization, storage, and use.

Centrally located collections are most effective, as this promotes efficient use of space (particularly in terms of combining preparation and work areas). However, it may also be operationally efficient to split the collections among potential users (for example, the herbarium and insect collection going to Natural Resources for storage and use).

Branch or satellite collections are possible as long as proper preservation and security conditions are met, and the requisite work areas necessary for management and use are provided. Overall responsibility for documentation, preservation, and reporting should, however, remain vested in one curatorial lead position, no matter where branch collections are located.

Establishing Access, Use, and Management Policies

Access, use, and management policies define who can access the collections (both staff and public), what types of use are possible and under what conditions, and how the collections should be managed. Desired outcomes or products should be identified as well; for example, the type of services that are expected from the collections. Some examples include production of over-lays for buried utilities; production of CDs containing research done at the park; liberal access to botanical specimens for comparative studies; and inter-library loan services.

The park may wish to consider the use of focus group exercises to develop a number of park-specific documents, including a Role and Function Statement, for the combined collections. These would clearly state who is responsible for the development of a joint resource and how the museum program will function to serve park-wide goals. Access and use policies should be defined and implemented, and responsibilities for development, documentation, and management of the resource should be defined in a formal Position Description and associated performance standards. These objectives must be fully defined in writing if they are to be accomplished in fact.

Some recommendations to consider for developing and formalizing the park's management philosophy for archives, libraries, and museum collections are as follows:

- Create a focus group of senior staff representing all park administrative units to define what the collections should contain, how they should be managed and accessed most efficiently, and what products should be produced upon request.

- Define the role and function of the combined collections by formal statement, formal access policies, and formal methodologies for depositing collections material, archival information, and required literature into the collections.

- Assign responsibility for developing and managing the joint collections to a single administrative unit and individual using a formal Position Description and performance standards.

- Identify possible cooperative partnerships in the community with groups that hold common interests regarding the preservation and management of park resources.

Issue Statement

The achievement of best practices for archives management will benefit resources and promote accessibility to archives collections for staff and public use.

Background

Since the park's beginning, the staff, superintendents, and concessionaires of the North Cascades National Park Service Complex, along with Ebey's Landing National Historical Reserve and San Juan National Historical Park—which fall under NOCA's curatorial responsibility—have created an irreplaceable administrative and resource management record that chronicles the history of these unique places. This archives collection reveals a long legacy of human interaction with the environment. The archival collections' associations with key site-related individuals, groups, and events make them as central to the site as the park structures and the ecosystems around them.

Authors, educators, filmmakers, park staff, publishers, students, and the public use archival collections as source material for their research, interpretation, and works. Park archives and records also serve as legal evidence; as baseline data for resource management; as outreach information for interpretation, publications, web sites, and educational programs; and to further park knowledge and study. Archival materials include:

Personal papers and family papers, such as the papers of the park founder or site-associated eminent individual, site-associated family papers, and similar collections;

Organizational records, such as a Cooperating Association's records or those of early corporations, institutions, or groups who flourished on the park site;

Assembled manuscript collections, such as historic views of the park site assembled by visitors or donors, or manuscripts that document site-associated events, activities, places, structures, ecosystem, or staff;

Resource management records, including NPS and contractor-generated records used to manage cultural and natural resources; field notes of an anthropological, archeological, or natural history field, interview, or excavation data; architectural or landscape records; cartographic materials; electronic/magnetic materials (such as audiotapes, CD-ROMs, databases, magnetic tape, and GIS data); moving images (including videotapes, motion pictures, and research footage); photographs (including negatives, transparencies, slides, prints, and direct positive processes such as daguerreotypes and tintypes); textual records (including Collection Management Plans, master plans, and research data), and similar items;

Administrative history records, including files accumulated for administrative history publications; desk files of individuals; subject files maintained for internal use; copies of internal policies; reference files of park ephemera; and copies of reports such as the superintendent's reports;

Individual manuscripts, including individual book manuscripts, electronic records, unpublished reports, correspondence, diaries, letters, lists, notes, and similar materials.

Archives and manuscript collections are mandated by legislation, regulations, and policy to be a part of the park's museum collection. Thus historically, museum approaches have often been applied to archival collections. However, archival collections require a distinct approach to ensure their integrity.

Six federal laws provide the basic legal mandate for managing museum collections in the NPS. Legislation began with the Act for the Preservation of American Antiquities of 1906, and continued with the Organic Act of 1916, the Historic Sites Act of 1935, the Museum Properties Management

Act of 1955, the National Historic Preservation Act of 1966, and the Archeological Resources Protection Act of 1979. Together these mandates laid the foundations for the protection and preservation of historic resources, including sites, buildings, objects, associated records, and reference materials.

The Historic Sites, Buildings, and Antiquities Act of 1935 was the first acknowledgement of the importance of records associated with specific artifacts. Associated records, such as drawings, plans, and photographs, provided valuable supporting data in the operation and management of historic and archaeological sites, buildings, and objects.

The National Historic Preservation Act of 1966 (NHPA), as amended through 1992, reasserted the authority of park museums over historical documents. Section 110 of this act called for the preservation of any historic property owned or controlled by a federal agency, including records. The NHPA required that "records and other data, including data produced by historical research and archeological surveys and excavations are permanently maintained in appropriate databases and made available to potential users."

The Archaeological Resources Protection Act (ARPA) of 1979 further made it compulsory that records associated with an archeological project be maintained as an integral part of the collection. In fact, associated records such as field notes, photos, and maps can make up an entire collection, particularly when survey projects do not yield material remains.

Regulations establishing the standards, procedures, and guidelines for the preservation of recovered prehistoric and historic material and their associated records are outlined in Title 36 of the Code of Federal Regulations Part 79 - *Curation of Federally-Owned and Administered Archaeological Collections* (36 CFR 79). This regulation focuses attention on the importance of records associated with archeological projects, and on the records resulting from the management of archeological projects. It also broadens the scope of curation service beyond artifacts and their associated records.

Curatorial services now include managing and preserving a collection in accordance with professional museum and archival practices. The practices listed in the regulations, however, are those broadly applicable to both the museum curation and archival professions. These, for example, include inventorying, accessioning, labeling, storing the collections using appropriate containers, and conserving the collections. The regulations do not address the specialized techniques required of archival collections. Further, the regulations focus solely on the procedural aspect of archival work. While the use of archival quality materials, description, and finding aids is important in the overall processing of an archival collection, this is only one aspect of archival work. Recognition must also be given to the guiding principles of provenance and original order, which underpin archival appraisal and collection organization.

National Park Service policies implementing the above mandates and regulations are contained within DO#28: *Cultural Resources Management Guideline* and the NPS *Museum Handbook.*

Currently, the NPS recognizes the importance of treating archives in accordance with professional archival principles. The current *Museum Handbook* clearly demonstrates this in the following passage: "Archival and manuscript collections are museum collections, and they will be cataloged, preserved, arranged, and described in finding aids in ways that preserve the collections and their context (provenance and original order) intact while providing controlled access. With few legal exemptions, the NPS will make archives and manuscripts available to researchers . . . All documentation associated with natural and cultural resource studies and other resource management actions will be retained in the park's museum collection for use in managing park resources over time."

Archival and manuscript collections warrant specialized attention and adherence to professional practices that protect the collections' integrity. Even though National Park Service policy and guidelines regarding archival and manuscript collections are aligning with professional archival principles, implementation relies on the training and ability of the museum staff.

Discussion

According to the 2003 Collection Management Report, North Cascades National Park has custody of 74,625 archival items in its museum collection, 52,367 of which have been cataloged into the Automated National Catalog System (ANCS+) Collection Management Module. An inventory by the NOCA curator shows a substantial backlog of 359 linear feet or 574,400 items of archival material. The Collection Management Report notes only 211 research requests for 2003, but this does not reflect the actual use of the park's archival and manuscript holdings by park staff and the public.

The curatorial staff at NOCA has worked hard and devoted considerable time, energy, and attention to the archival collections. Unfortunately, most of the archival work did not proceed according to standard archival procedures. Consequently, several problems have emerged that are serious, though not insurmountable.

The physical and intellectual arrangement of the collections needs to be improved. The provenance of some collections is unclear, the hierarchical levels of arrangement within collections are confusing or non-existent, and logical arrangement schemes are seldom identified or employed.

Problems with cataloging and description are partly the result of failure to comprehend the internal organizational structure of collections. Most of the archival holdings at NOCA already are arranged *physically* into distinct collections, although this physical segregation is not always reflected in the ANCS+ catalog entries. On the other hand, there are also many individual documents that not only have been cataloged inappropriately as individual museum objects but which physically are part of ill-defined or unarranged collections, and are mixed with documents that could belong to other collections.

Cataloged documents in the ANCS+ Collection Management Module have mostly been entered incorrectly at the series level, or the file unit level, or even the item level, instead of the collection level. In the Collection Management Module the actual descriptions and even the titles tend to be sketchy, and often fail to convey much meaningful information. Photograph collections, while accessioned as discrete collections, are item-cataloged in the Collection Management Module with each photograph assigned a catalog number and incorrectly documented as historical rather than archival.

The finding aids are inconsistent, not created to discipline standards and consist of indexes inserted into the storage boxes, printed inventory sheets, and a Microsoft Access database detailing inventory description. In addition, some items may have been accessioned into the museum collection inappropriately, and would be more suitable for the park library or for a curatorial reference collection.

A professionally trained and experienced archivist needs to conduct an archival assessment and survey of the park. The purpose of the survey is to make a comprehensive and systematic review of official and non-official archival holdings. The survey is intended to assist park staff in making decisions about record groups that would be appropriate for inclusion in the museum collection. The focus of the survey is upon collection level descriptions, including appraisal, evaluation, and recommendations for arrangement and description (accessioning, cataloging, finding aid production, and web-based collection level descriptions).

Secondary information will consist of three reviews: 1) preservation condition of the record groups examined (prioritized needs for stabilization, re-housing, reformatting, and treatment); 2) potential legal problems (copyright, privacy/publicity concerns); and 3) a summary of existing problems in the park infrastructure for archives (such as missing policies and procedures, and the adequacy of the Scope of Collection Statement, equipment, space, staff training, and staffing). The results of the survey and the short and long range planning suggestions provided in the survey report will provide guidance to the park in setting priorities for accessioning, processing, cataloging, preserving, and providing access to park archival collections.

Archives Management

While the functions of museum and archives are similar, the approach each discipline takes to accomplish these functions is fundamentally different. Many museum employees report that appraising, arranging, and describing archival collections presents the greatest difficulty. Archival methodologies can provide curators with good guidance in the appropriate approaches to these tasks. The following sections will discuss the selection process including acquisition and appraisal of documents, and intellectual access including arranging, cataloging, and describing collections. A discussion of preservation and reference services will follow.

Acquisition and Appraisal

The acquisition process includes identifying material that falls within the scope of collections, appraising materials for permanent value, and assuming legal custody through the accession process. The park's mission, as stated in the enabling legislation, presidential proclamation, or executive order, guides the scope of a park's museum acquisitions. According to the *Museum Handbook,* "acquisition methods for museum objects include: gift, purchase, exchange, transfer, field collection, and loan." Archives typically acquire a group of related records to serve as the park's institutional memory.

Before formal acquisition can take place, staff must appraise the materials' value to determine which are to be retained as archives. Appraisal is one of the most critical aspects of archival work. The primary purpose of an archives is to sustain a collective memory and communicate that memory to future generations. Appraising archival collections involves not just the consideration of historical issues, but also requires a firm understanding of the value of records for accountability and evidence.

Archivists appraise primary sources, in contrast to curators' appraisal of specimens and objects which is largely guided by the intrinsic rarity or representative value of each piece. Archivists must not only judge whether specific collections are relevant to a park's scope of collections, they must also judge the secondary value of records that document the "big picture."

If a collection or document is appraised as not having archival value, that information is forever lost.

When appraising records, archivists must be especially sound in their analysis of the organization and functioning body with which they deal, and they must have a broad knowledge of probable research need and interest. Archivists judge the value of the item in relation to other items, that is, in relation to the entire documentation of the activity that resulted in its production. Therefore, they select records for preservation in the aggregate, not as single items. The collection provides context to its individual parts. When each archival document is viewed as an object the concept of records being inter-related with one another is not respected.

In general, the current NOCA system for acquisition and appraisal of archival collections is not functioning in accordance with archival theory and methodology. Park museum staff have been doing their best to execute these functions, but the contradictory nature of museums and archives methods makes satisfying these tasks difficult. Decentralization of resource management records into the park archives has expanded archival holdings, thus increasing the demands on museum staff.

At present, NOCA archives has much unnecessary material, and lacks records and manuscripts that should have been acquired. Furthermore, many accessioned collections lack provenance, original order, and are typically organized as smaller pieces of what was once a large collection. The current budget and staffing situations require archival acquisitions to be highly scrutinized. NOCA museum staff needs much support, training and guidance in performing the delicate and demanding task of appraisal.

Arranging, Cataloging, and Describing

Archivists, curators, and librarians all desire to make their holdings accessible for research. In order to provide users physical access to holdings, there must first be intellectual access. Each discipline is guided by different principles to provide access to their specific materials. With regard to archives, intellectual access is provided through the arrangement and description of the archival collection. Archives preserve and make accessible the documentary resources park administrators need for successful operations. Archives also support ongoing resource management projects and serve the research needs of park employees and the public. In order for these responsibilities to be met, proper cataloging of archival collections is vital. Employing non-archival arranging, cataloging, and describing methods can compromise the integrity of an archival collection.

Figure 1 - Archivist Robert Applegate in NOCA archives storage

Archival descriptive practice includes cataloging and the production of finding aids. Archivists catalog collections at multiple levels with emphasis on the provenance and function of non-published, usually unique groups of materials. Archival cataloging captures the contents and structure, the context, the conditions for access and use, and the linked materials relating to their holdings.

Archivists base the complexity and detail of an archival description upon the value of the collection. They give relatively minimal descriptions to collections with less monetary value and risk, fewer users, and less evidential, associational, and artifactual information. Collections with greater value, risk, and usage receive fuller or more detailed description at more levels.

All park archival descriptive work begins at the collection level. Minimal records are preliminary data most frequently gained during surveying. Full records are the standard data elements sought for an average collection that fits a park's Scope of Collection Statement (SOCS) and has at least moderate value and/or usage. Archivists produce detailed or in-depth catalog records only for the most significant archival holdings in a park. Archivists start by gathering minimal information for planning and minimal cataloging during a survey. Only after processing do archivists produce full or detailed catalog records.

The size and complexity of archival collections require archivists to describe the collections and their context hierarchically, moving from the general to the specific. Archivists describe collections at a variety of levels, beginning at the broadest, or collection, level. The data fields used at the various levels may vary. At each of these, the level of descriptive detail will differ, but are based upon a wide array of standards, including those established by international, national, and professional organizations and the NPS MMP standards specific to ANCS+.

Archival cataloging techniques are complex and professionally standardized. To develop the necessary skills requires experience, training, and an apprenticeship under a trained professional. Using untrained or inexperienced catalogers ensures that the work will not meet professional standards. Many older ANCS+ catalog records will require significant revision, particularly field contents, field authority usage, and Archives Personal Papers and Manuscript (APPM) stylistic formatting. Poor archival cataloging records don't provide good accountability and access to collections or meet any of the other basic purposes of archival cataloging.

Preservation and Reference Services

Preservation entails safeguarding the physical integrity of material through repairing, restoring, maintaining, or protecting documents. Archivists may use reformatting techniques for preservation to retain the information contained on a document, not necessarily the document itself. For instance, highly acidic and unstable diazotype maps are often reformatted onto microfilm or digitized, in order to remove the original which may degrade other materials.

The final and foremost function of archives is to provide users with reference services so they may have physical access to the facilities holdings. As public institutions, parks have a legal obligation to provide physical access and reference services. The Organic Act of 1916 mandates that agency collections are to be preserved and maintained for the use and enjoyment of the American people. The Freedom of Information Act (FOIA) provides U.S. citizens with unrestricted access to the documentary records of the actions of their government, such as policy files. In addition, federal agencies must provide swift access to FOIA requests.

However, not all government records are open to the public. Certain personnel files, internal personnel practices, records compiled for law enforcement, archeological records that reveal site locations, and records documenting the nature of archeological resources are legally exempt from FOIA requests. Therefore, privacy issues must be considered before providing access and reference services to the public. Responding quickly to all research inquires whether they are by telephone, mail, e-mail, or in person is important to maintaining a positive rapport with the public. Providing proper reference services is difficult with limited staff and designated space for research. Adequate supervision is vital to ensure the preservation and safety of the National Park Service's collections, as well as copyright and privacy protections.

Records Management

Numerous NOCA/EBLA cultural, natural, resource, and administrative staff members interviewed during research for this document have committed themselves to the retention of resource-related documentation, but there is much confusion and lack of direction. Often these records are thoughtlessly purged because of a weak emphasis on professional records management—resource related records in particular—within the NPS. Methods for improving park records management activities should be provided for staff, in addition to archival guidance for the museum collection.

The value of a well-organized park museum archives cannot be underestimated or understated. It serves as a source of cultural, natural, interpretive, and planning research and data, reflecting past management decisions and serving as the basis for current and future management decisions. Thorough recording of past resource projects prevents needless repetition of studies, as has been common in the NPS's past. Retaining past park management documents also serves as legal protection for park staff when issues arise that hinge on past park actions. Many issues critical to a park are revisited over its history, so the history of the park's actions is vital to understanding the present and future forces affecting the park.

Records management training is available to NPS employees, although often from other federal agencies. The staff management should contact the Pacific West Region/Seattle Office training officer for further assistance in locating appropriate training opportunities for park staff. A NOCA records management officer should contact the NPS service-wide records officer, Michael Grimes (202-208-4333) for all the reference material needed to perform record management activities.

The NOCA management staff should establish a records review policy. The designated park records manager should establish a records disposition board, involving all park divisions and sites, to review all records before formal disposition by the records officer. The park will then have the opportunity to ensure the retention of important documents pertaining to the park's mission: records of park resource management, of the history of interpretation of the park's resources, and of park archeological and historical research projects. This board would also establish, through the input of the park curator, an SOP delineating the proper transfer of permanent material to the museum archives (see Appendix A, page 85). It will also ensure that ineligible records, such as personnel related documents containing personal data protected under the Privacy Act, will not be incorporated into the park archives.

Recommendations

- Conduct an archival assessment/survey of parks and sites under NOCA's umbrella of curatorial responsibility. Obtain funds and contact professional NPS archives personnel.

- Establish clear procedures for retiring resource management records to the park archives. Establish lines of communication with park divisions and provide guidance documents/SOP to facilitate the transfer of material (see Appendix A, page 85).

- Establish a records disposition board involving all park divisions and sites to dictate park records policy and to review all records before formal disposition by the records officer.

- Initiate training to change how employees view records management and to spark interest and commitment to proper recordkeeping practices.

- Review current museum object and archives management staffing needs in light of the present and future museum curation workload Ensure positions are filled by qualified professionals on base (ONPS) funding and provide continuing education for staff professionals.

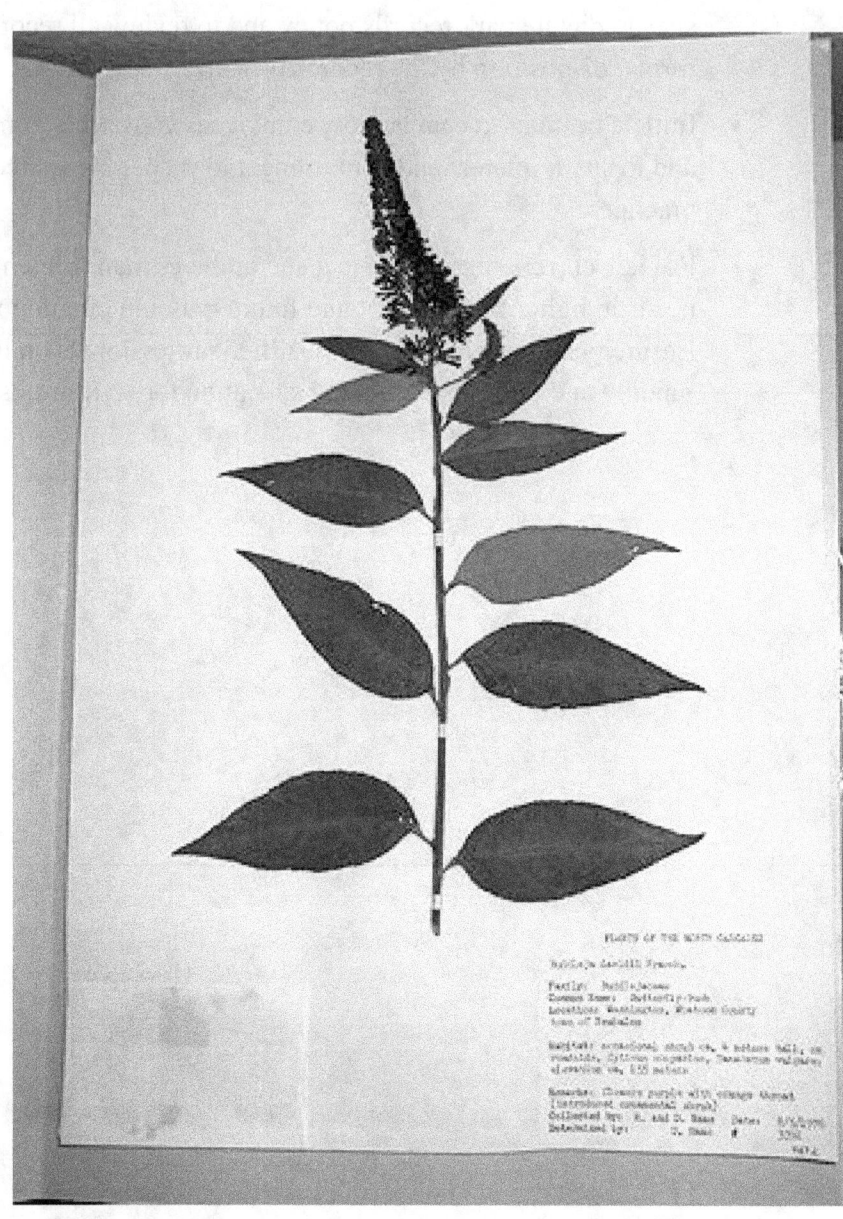

Figure 2   Herbarium specimen with label

North Cascades National Park Service Complex Museum Management Plan

Issue Statement

Existing park collections must be better documented and organized to be of maximum supportive use to park programs, while protocols and standards need to be formalized to govern collection growth.

Background

The history of collections has been summarized in the introductory section of this document. It touches on the relationships of the issues concerning the increase in the number and quality of the scientific collection. Most of the concerns focus on directed growth and the improvement of the scientific collection through subsequent use, research and culling. This section concentrates on the current status of those collections that have resulted from formal research. It also discusses information that continues to be collected during data recovery expeditions and baseline data forays, and information that could eventually be incorporated into a research design.

The North Cascades natural history collections are housed at Marblemount Curation Facility, Newhalem Research Center, The Burke Museum, and the University of Washington herbarium. The arrangements with the University of Washington are likely to continue for the foreseeable future since significant research and inventorying projects are being cooperatively conducted by NPS staff and University of Washington professors and students.

The collection storage room at Stehekin will house natural history objects, such as the entomological specimens that have been collected, plus those that are likely to be collected and prepared through the park Inventory and Monitoring Program. Ebey's Landing (EBLA) and San Juan Island National Historical Park (SAJH) will also have voucher specimens housed at the Marblemount Curation Facility and the University of Washington herbarium after they are collected, prepared, and annotated. EBLA has no natural science specimens in its collection, but this is likely to change as the Inventory and Monitoring (I&M) Program begins to intensify collecting there. EBLA does not have space dedicated to an herbarium.

Relatively few vertebrate specimens have been collected and prepared from NOCA. The collection is comprised of 220 vertebrate species that are housed at the Burke Museum as comparative samples for research. Park personnel currently have no plan to add preserved specimens to the collection; however, active invertebrate collecting is being conducted in the park. This collecting program began as part of the Federal Energy Regulatory Commission (FERC) re-licensing agreement and is now part of the Inventory and Monitoring program.

SUBJECT	TYPE	NOCA	EBLA	SAJH		
				BURKE	MCF	FOVA
Archeology		3,624	1,800	71,526	27,509	5,727
Biology		9,994		21	494	
Geology		1,303			28	
Paleontology		4			39	
History		1657			1058	
Archives		275	1	14	31	

Table 1 Number of cataloged records in each facility associated with NOCA, EBLA, and SAJH collections

Geological field schools have been conducted within the North Cascades park boundaries for decades. These field schools have been tracked through the permit system, which has allowed them to house the collections though the information is entered into ANCS+. Glacier monitoring and geological landform mapping are being conducted by NPS staff. These projects generate data, maps, field notes, and photos that will become part of the park collection once the projects become inactive.

The cultural collections include objects that document history, archeology, ethnography, and associated records from each of the park units. The majority of objects come from archeological investigations. Overall, the archeological artifacts have accurate provenance and are associated with good site descriptions and other information that meets federal and state documentation standards. The history objects have varied research value because some lack many of the necessary associated records. Few park funded ethnographic documentation projects have been carried out, but the data is adequately recorded and stored at the Marblemount Curation Facility. Ethnographic research has been done by other institutions. While the information from these documents may not pertain directly to the park, background data on affiliated tribes could be useful in land-use studies.

The Thomas Burke Museum of Natural History and Culture at the University of Washington houses prehistoric artifacts and the original associated records from San Juan Island's English Camp excavations. This collection has been fully processed and cataloged into the Burke cataloging system ARGUS as well as into ANCS+. The Marblemount Curation Facility houses the historic artifacts and original associated records from all San Jan Island excavations.

Since the Burke-housed artifacts and specimens have been analyzed for the final report and now offer value to researchers as a comparative collection, they have been arranged by type instead of by provenance. Samples from each facies and stratum are housed according to their material or genus, making it possible for researchers to look at several objects of the same grouping. While this is tremendously useful for identification projects, the specimens are not housed to accommodate researchers interested in general intra-site analysis. Researchers interested in revisiting on-site associations will have to rely on the associated records instead of the objects to address their questions. The majority of the artifacts housed at the Burke are shell samples but a there is also a significant amount of bone and lithic material. Many of the sediment samples have undergone chemical analysis and that data is recorded in several publications.

Discussion

The responsibilities of the North Cascades curator have increased over the past several years with the addition of collections from parks within the

North Coast and Cascades Network. This has been a positive movement that bolsters the credibility of the facility as a research center for the network. However, with the changing of personnel and the restructuring of how park programs conduct business, it is imperative that the curator be involved in aspects of the planning process for all scientific activities and monitoring programs taking place in the parks served by the collections. The curator's involvement also must extend to each project's close-out to ensure that appropriate materials are transferred to the facility and included in the permanent files. This level of involvement will require that the curator's position be upgraded to full-time, a conclusion discussed in greater detail in Issue F.

Inventory and Monitoring Program

The NPS Natural Resource Challenge is responsible for providing the Natural Resource Divisions in the network with a direction that focuses on Inventory and Monitoring resources within the park. Although NPS-77 states that the Inventory and Monitoring data systems are meant only to track data, many of the projects generate specimens and records documenting National Park Service resources that will be preserved in the curation facility. A major aspect of the I&M program is the appointment of data management positions to track and coalesce information in a standardized format (i.e. GIS shapefiles, reports, databases, photos, spreadsheets, and notes) to be included in the NatureBib and NPSpecies.

The data manager position is an important link for the curator to fully understand which I&M projects are generating valuable data and specimens that fit with the Scope of Collections and should be transferred to collection storage. The Marblemount Curation Facility should function as a storage area for I&M backup data, as well as the park facility that houses archived copies of reports and information. With the sensitivity of much of the I&M data, this information and associated specimens need to fall under a restricted access category. Data managers need to remain the contact for any inquiries about the I&M information.

The data manager position has similar responsibilities to the North Cascades curator as a multi-park manager. This similarity should make the exchange of information between the programs seamless. At North Cascades National Park Service Complex, the data manager is the recipient of I&M project information conducted at Ebey's Landing and San Juan as well as North Cascades. While North Cascades and San Juan have easily identifiable park boundaries, Ebey's Landing National Historical Reserve poses some difficulty in determining what constitutes NPS property for origins of collections. This is because the I&M projects cover the entire Reserve and specimens might not have been collected from NPS property. While the information will be owned by the NPS, none of the specimens will be tracked in the NPS Museum Catalog system.

This issue is most notable in botany forays and the existing agreement with the University of Washington herbarium. The agreement between the NPS and the herbarium states that, when possible, three specimens will be collected and prepared for the herbarium at Marblemount, UW, and another off-site location that has yet to be determined. Once the specimens have been prepared, the NPS will transfer ownership of the specimens to institutions that hold them. If NPS-permitted the collector determines that only one specimen should be collected, the primary repository will be at the University of Washington because of its ability to better accommodate researchers. A clause in the agreement also allows for the NPS to decide not to transfer threatened and endangered specimens in order to retain control over the dissemination of information regarding the location of that species. Aspects of this agreement still appear to be open for discussion and will not be covered in this MMP.

As recommended by the curator, both the data manager and research advisor concur that the I&M data manager meetings would be a solid avenue for the curator to gain insight into the data handling topics being discussed at the network level as well as how the I&M program meshes with the museum program. The transfer of materials to the curation facility may first appear as a trivial detail since I&M data is backed up in another clearinghouse, but over a longer period of time the consistency of placing material in the curation facility will benefit the park. An obvious benefit is that the objects and their associated records will be preserved in a stable environment and will allow future researchers to build on this generation's findings.

The curator and data manager need to develop in-house procedures that define what I&M data will be transferred to the Marblemount Curation Facility. The level of data significance also needs to be addressed in the procedures so that incomplete or unnecessary data does not get cataloged into the museum system.

Permits

The permitting process service-wide has been difficult to manage in large part because of the time and funding necessary to appoint staff to act as a liaison between the park curator and the researcher. North Cascades, Ebey's Landing, and San Juan are no different. A research advisor at North Cascades is involved with the permitting process, but research projects often take several years to complete. Many researchers do not have a solid understanding of catalog data requirements, year-end summary reports, and collection ownership by the NPS.

In the past, each approved permit from the park was assigned an accession number for research data and objects that were expected to be incorporated into the overall collection. Some proposed research projects that were assigned permits were never started and did not generate any material. Consequently there was nothing to accession except the permit. This approach has changed so that accession numbers are now used peripherally for permit tracking. While the past approach may have been intended to keep the curator informed, the new approach will require a more active role.

The curator's role should include assessing what projects will generate material and act in some cases as park liaison responsible for contacting researchers concerning the transfer and storage of material. This active role is necessary to maintain some control over the condition in which material is delivered for curation. Curator involvement would make sure the park receives its property according to standards, and alleviate confusion researchers may have concerning their responsibilities.

The curator and the research advisor concur that the network's Permit Committee meetings would also benefit from curator involvement. An appropriate committee meeting agenda item would be the development of standard operating procedures for the network on how to address park curation needs and define how best to communicate those needs to the researcher.

Compliance

Other documentation projects not funded by the I&M program are likely to be conducted by park staff. This is especially true of cultural resource projects conducted for Section 106 and 110 compliance or for other inventory purposes. All NOCA compliance projects are tracked at North Cascades Headquarters, with a checklist of personnel who need to be involved and informed for each project. Neither the curator, nor the chief of cultural resources, nor the archeologist are listed as members of the Interdisciplinary Team (IDT). This information chain is not the best way to keep the curator updated on projects that may result in collection growth. While much of the IDT discussions concentrate on overall compliance and logistics, a well defined route should exist for the curator to find out what compliance projects will generate objects for the collection. This is needed not only for the planning and general management of the curation facilities, but also to ensure these projects are fully documented. An easy solution to the planning issue would be to include the curator as a signatory to the project clearance requests.

Compliance at San Juan and Ebey's Landing are more difficult to track at North Cascades since those park units act independently and usually use regional staff to clear their compliance projects. Also, no trained cultural resource field staff are located at the island parks to act as liaison between park activities and the curator. Both parks instead have resource staff responsible for informing the curator of projects that generate objects for the collection. This may be the clearest route for information to travel from the outlying parks to the curator, but better defined methods for these communication lines need to be outlined for the resource staff. Another approach would be to include the North Cascades curator as a signatory along with the regional reviewers.

Archeology Records

At North Cascades the archeology collection is likely to increase over the next few years due to salvage efforts during the Stehekin Road compliance and the Ross Lake Site data recovery project. While previous park survey projects have yielded few objects, the associated records such as field notes, photographs, maps, and site records are currently being processed. Some of these original records date back to the earliest park surveys and are beginning to deteriorate. For instance, field notes and maps that were written in pencil are being smudged because they have been used for references during following surveys.

The Society of American Archaeologists lists the preservation of field notes as valuable primary data that require archival care, and that archeologists are responsible for ensuring that associated records are preserved. None of the three parks do this adequately. While the development of standard operating procedures could provide a roadmap for archeologists to follow in order to meet the record preservation requirements (see Issue A), a task force that includes network archeologists, curators, and regional staff needs to be formed to address the problem of missing or deteriorating field notes and records.

Archeology Collection Culling

Volume and preservation are problems in some of the existing collections. While the natural resource collection expansion appears to be thoughtful and controlled at this time, archeology collections will require attention in the near future.

The archeology collections generated from surveys within North Cascades are generally well organized and maintained. These collections have been processed in a uniform way and are separated using the Smithsonian trinomial, making it easy to locate artifacts intuitively. As in all archeology collections, oversized bulk samples are housed separately. But the location information is accurate so this does not pose any significant problems with the North Cascades archeology collection.

However, the two collections generated during compliance projects at Ebey's Landing were collected without guidance from a Scope of Collection Statement for the park. Initially every object that was in the dirt was retained because the sediment was inspected by trail crew members instead of archeologists. The idea during this phase in the testing was that the objects would be sorted in the laboratory.

Since historical archeologists from Fort Vancouver were the primary investigators during the second phase of testing, guidance from the Fort Vancouver collecting philosophy was used for all historic material. Many of the artifacts that were collected do not have stratigraphic provenance, and other objects, especially the metal, are deteriorating despite being housed in a stable environment. While the historic artifacts have been analyzed, the prehistoric artifacts and fire cracked rocks have yet to be studied and the sediment and botanical samples are not fully processed. This project is expected to be completed during fiscal year 2005. During the collaborative report writing period, the archeologists involved with the Ferry House compliance and testing project need to consult with the curator to determine how much of the artifactual material should be retained in the collection.

San Juan archeology also has problems from over-collecting during the University of Washington archeology field school at English Camp. Field Operation D, an excavation block outside of the parade ground, is particularly oversized because collection methods were altered during the excavation season. The field directors opted to excavate more area with less processing in the field with the assumption that culling would happen in the laboratory during analysis.

While much of the English Camp prehistoric material resides at the Burke, the Marblemount Curation Facility currently houses the historic artifacts and the bulk samples from the shell midden. The bulk samples take up a significant amount of space. This issue was recognized even during the time that the Burke Museum was storing them. The principal investigator and Burke collections manager listed what tasks need to be accomplished to make the collection ready for analysis and noted that the bulk samples could be significantly reduced. This plan of action needs to be revisited with input for culling from the principal investigator (see Appendix C, page 101).

The University of Idaho-excavated collections of historic material from San Juan sites are harder to address concerning culling because they have all been processed, analyzed and properly housed. This issue tends to pit the preservation and research philosophy of archeologists against the preservation and operation philosophy of curators and collection managers. The topic is broached in a discussion paper *Proactive Management of Archeological Collections* (Appendix C) written by PWR Curator, Kent Bush. He states, "We have come to the point, however, where we need to be looking closely at what has been retained in the past, and what we want to retain in the future…" One of the suggested actions in the paper is, "archeological collections… need to be reviewed by a curator and archeologist team to determine whether the archeological collections at any given park could be improved, made more efficient, by judicial de-accessioning activities."

The collection of historic material from the San Juan sites offers an opportunity to develop some collecting protocols that may have application to this service-wide issue. While this may not be an immediate need for the operations of the North Cascades Marblemount Curation Facility, the basic truth is that the collections will continue to grow and that adequate storage space will be at a premium. This issue will be discussed in greater detail in the following section.

Recommendations

- Develop in-house procedures for the I&M specimens and records that outline employee responsibilities, collections transfer schedules, and criteria for project completion and data significance.

- Develop standard operating procedures for the network that address curation of specimen collections. Include this as an agenda item at upcoming Permit Committee meetings and involve the park curator in these meetings.

- Include the curator as a signatory to the North Cascades project clearance requests and to the Assessment of Effect (Triple X) forms for EBLA and SAJH.

- Create a task force that includes network archeologists, curators, and regional staff to address the pervasive problem of inadequate care for primary records.

- Process, assess, and cull the archaeology collections from EBLA and SAJH working with subject matter experts and principal investigators.

- Make the park curator a full member of the IDT Team.

Figure 3   San Juan Island historic archeology artifacts in storage

Issue Statement

Continued investment in the organization and growth of museum storage and work facilities is essential to the effective preservation and use of park museum object and archive collections.

Background

Adequate facilities for museum collections, including storage, work areas, and offices are critical for the professional management of these resources and their security and preservation. The National Park Service has established functional standards for museum spaces, as contained in the Checklist for Preservation and Protection of Museum Spaces. North Cascade's investment in museum facilities has been an ongoing success and has provided museum space justified by the size and nature of its museum collections and operations.

Museum facilities at North Cascades Complex consist of three storage locations and work spaces. The primary museum operation and storage is located at Marblemount where a facility was built (in the early 1990s) to house museum collections, work and laboratory space, and offices for the curator, chief of cultural resources, and archeological staff. The Newhalem Research Station is a research laboratory that also houses natural science specimens under development or actively used for research. The third storage location is in the basement of the recently renovated Golden West Lodge in the Stehekin district of Lake Chelan National Recreation Area.

Marblemount

The Marblemount curatorial building was under construction during the site visit of the 1994 Collection Management Plan. Various recommendations about the layout of the facility by the planning team were made and implemented. The facility appears to have had no major problems in its design or maintenance over the years, and is capable of meeting or exceeding most standards for the storage of museum collections. The rooms within the Marblemount curatorial facility are:

Laboratory	10 x 25 ft.	NOCA Room	19 x 35 ft.
Supplies Storage	5 x 10 ft.	SAJU Room	25 x 38 ft.
Loading Storage	12 x 12 ft.	Processing	12 x 19 ft.
Work Area	15 x 31 ft.	Restroom	6 x 10 ft.
Offices (3)	10 x 10 ft.	Curator Office	9 x 11 ft.

Table 2 Marblemount rooms and sizes

The main storage room, currently called the NOCA room, is 665 square feet and has cabinets mounted on movable carriages consisting of six double-sided movable rows and one single-sided fixed end-row. An assessment was made of the present storage capacity of the movable cabinets, and out of 56 single-wide units, about 43% space remains for additional materials, or the equivalent of 24 cabinets. The capacity may appear to provide for many years of additional growth, except for the materials already waiting to be housed in cabinets. This includes the equivalent of about eight cabinets of geological specimens housed on the loading dock, which require processing and some culling before entering the NOCA room. The other materials awaiting re-housing into cabinets are 24 Buckhorn plastic boxes with geology specimens that are stored on top of the cabinets. All of this geology material will easily require a minimum of 10 cabinets storage space. Currently, the EBLA collections require less than one standard museum cabinet for storage.

The curator has been intensively involved in reorganizing the arrangement of materials within the Spacesaver cabinets. Goals include storing similar collections together and incorporating new collections into appropriate spaces.

Other collections in the NOCA room include the herbarium collection housed in six full-height and four half-height cabinets. Additional cabinets were purchased to accommodate the herbarium, as the standard for an herbarium cabinet is not to exceed 80% full, allowing adequate room for handling and some growth potential. Six half-height herbarium cabinets house the lichen and moss collections, and they average about 50% capacity at this time. An entomology cabinet has two drawers with insects; only about 10% of this cabinet is now in use. An unusual double-ended, no-door cabinet on wheels has various supplies and archeological reference collections. Its capacity was not reviewed as it does not represent quality storage space for permanent collections.

The new addition to the Marblemount facility was constructed in 2001 and it added 950 square feet to the existing building, specifically to house the San Juan Island archeological collections. This SAJH room has a movable-aisle storage system with 36 double-wide cabinets. A review of these cabinets placed their capacity at close to 100% capacity. The true number may be closer to 90%, given small amounts of space here and there that may be available, but for management purposes very little space is available for new collections. Some additional storage space is located in fixed cabinets housing records and other related materials. These shelves have a small amount of expansion space. The room also has 71 small, 106 medium, and 34 large Buckhorn boxes, suggesting that currently the room is at—or exceeds—its cabinet storage capacity.

The processing room contains two computer workstations, fire-resistant safes for museum records, refrigerator for film, and holding space for pre-accession processing. Forty boxes of archives for appraisal are currently being stored in this room. Little can be done to increase storage at this time—it is utilized to the maximum.

The environmental control system consists of a heat pump HVAC system and in-room dehumidifiers. The heat pump was upgraded in 2004 as the unit installed had too low a capacity and became overworked. The in-room dehumidifiers are also somewhat smaller than is needed and require manual removal of accumulated water.

The environment is monitored through the use of portable Datalogger units. In the past, hand-written spot recordings were made on log sheets. A large amount of Datalogger data was lost during a cyclic replacement of a desktop computer system when the data was not retrieved prior to computer replacement. Some printouts of this data survive, and allow some review of the environmental parameters within storage.

Newhalem Research Station

This facility is located in a Seattle City Light building that has recently undergone renovation and contains a high-quality laboratory and collection storage. The space will be addressed in this plan as a museum facility. Its access and control are the responsibility of scientists and resource managers, and most of the space is used for scientific lab work. The wet specimens and other materials stored here are housed in new museum specimen cabinets that meet or exceed service standards.

Environmental data for the station was analyzed in 2002 in a document titled "Environmental History" (no source given). It addresses the problem of 12 degree fluctuation in temperature and 35% relative humidity (RH) fluctuation on a daily basis. After turning off the HVAC system, fluctuations dropped substantially to 3° F and 23% RH. While noting that the RH was still too high, it pointed to needed improvements for the mechanical system. After filter changes and the addition of heater components, the system performed much better. The control of the environment in this space is considered the most important consideration for the protection of the specimens, and should continue to be monitored.

Stehekin

The Golden West Lodge was constructed in 1927-28, some of it using parts from an even older building. By the 1990s the building was in need of major rehabilitation, which was completed in 2003. A room in the basement level has been designed and constructed as the museum storage room. It contains 350 sq. ft. in a single room with air conditioning, fire alarm, and sprinklers. At the time of the team visit, it was close to completion but still under construction with the floor covering yet to be laid. A variety of museum objects and some shelving and cabinets were stored there; storage equipment has yet to be installed. A plan for the access to this space ensures clearly defined security in this remote district. Occasionally, especially in the winter season, different staff members may be absent for long periods of time. The NOCA curator currently visits the district perhaps a total of two weeks annually. Adding moveable-aisle system cabinets to this room is justified for securing the objects before expansion space is needed.

Discussion

The Marblemount curatorial building needs additional investment in staff time and funds to maintain the environment to NPS standards and maximize the efficient use of available space. The park should consider purchasing new dehumidifiers that can handle larger amounts of air humidity and can operate without manual water removal. Waterless systems such as Bry-Air units, or the installation of drainage tubes that can carry water away from the units directly to drain pipes will remedy this. Monitoring of all museum spaces should be continued, and equipment modernized to make data collection as automated as possible.

The curator should continue to incorporate new collections and reorganize storage to maximize effective use of the space. Some culling of archives and archeology might free additional space, as discussed elsewhere in this plan. However, projects are also already identified that will generate new collections, perhaps of some substantial volumes (see Issues A and B on archives and scientific collections respectively).

Within the five year planning scope of this plan it can be expected that the park will need to begin to plan and seek funding for a new addition to the Marblemount facility. The original facility cost $100,000 in 1992. The new addition required $ 208,000 in funding just two years ago for 950 sq. ft. At this point the planning team assumes that a 1,000 sq. ft. addition sometime in this decade will be justified by collections growth. At an estimated $250 per sq. ft. for construction, the cost will be in the neighborhood of $250,000. It may be possible to enlarge the facility even more, but the park should perform an analysis on the maximum size for this facility in a historic district before the building grows substantially in its footprint.

The museum storage room at the Golden West Lodge is an important addition to the protection of objects and archives in the Stehekin District. This remote site justifies the need for this small but useful satellite of the museum program. The room needs to be reorganized in order to provide the zones of physical access appropriate to the user. The NOCA curator, and perhaps the park's cultural resource manager, would have full access to all the collections. Other users might require access only to the general storage area (the front area near the door) to access the room's environmental controls, to place pre-accession materials in the room for evaluation (such as boxes of park records), or to check on the overall security and well-being of the room itself after periods of power failure or snow melt. Emergency personnel might require access through a break box located at a central location for a one-time access.

A series of discussions and meetings should be held to discuss all possible needs and permutations of access throughout the year. This appears to be exceptionally challenging during the winter when staffing levels are at their minimum and staff are sometimes gone for long periods of time, making it hard to predict which people will be in charge of the building. Whatever procedures are developed must be clear and adaptable, so they will ensure maintenance of safe and appropriate access controls.

Recommendations

- Purchase and install dehumidification equipment suitable to the space that does not require manual draining.

- Consider installing hard-wired dataloggers linked to a computer that automatically collects environmental data.

- Continue to upgrade storage cabinets and shelving, replacing old, inadequate, or unsuitable units. Continue reorganization of storage for efficient space usage and access.

- Develop plans for a new addition to the Marblemount museum facility. Consider possible size, sites, and styles and complete compliance consultations well in advance of any funding. Request needed addition through PMIS.

- Continue environmental monitoring in all museum spaces, especially in the Newhalem Research Station. Upgrade equipment with digital equipment as funding allows.

- Complete the development of the museum room at the Golden West Lodge in Stehekin, including newly purchased cabinets and shelving. Consult on access needs and develop SOPs to address them realistically.

- Work with Island County Historical Museum regarding opportunities for EBLA collection management.

Figure 4   Backlog catalog storage

North Cascades National Park Service Complex Museum Management Plan

Issue Statement

Improvement of existing museum accession and catalog records will provide accountability and access to support collections use.

Background

Museum records in the National Park Service constitute the institutional knowledge essential to the use and protection of museum object and archive collections. They consist primarily of accession and catalog records, along with other program files on security, environment, and use. The North Cascades museum records were reviewed as part of this management plan, along with review of Ebey's Landing and San Juan Island catalog records.

Some understanding of NOCA museum records can be gained by referring to the "History of Museum Collections" section in this plan. The growth of museum collections inevitably involves gathering information on their source, identity, and condition. Much of the early growth of collections involved somewhat limited, and in some cases flawed, documentation of the objects and records. In perhaps the majority of instances, at least for historical collections, information on the source of creation and/or use was missing and little or nothing was documented about why artifacts were deemed worthy of accessioning.

Accession Records

Accessioning is the process of bringing objects into the park's museum collection and documenting their legal ownership and history or provenance. The decision to acquire museum collections involves an appraisal of whether the materials fit within the park's Scope of Collection

Statement (SOCS) and are worthy of preservation in perpetuity. The park has a draft SOCS that improves upon the current approved document.

Materials to be accessioned may be legally mandated to remain federal property, as is the case for archeological collections covered under the Archeological Resources Protection Act. Other materials, such as most historical artifacts, are discretionary as to whether they serve the mission of the park and should be acquired as permanent cultural property. Accessioning is perhaps the most essential step in documenting museum collections. Ensuring that the NPS has clear legal title can often be done only at the point of accessioning. Information on the provenance of materials is often obtained orally or through the context of acquisition. If it is not written out in the accession records, this information may be lost.

The NPS museum recordkeeping system is designed primarily for in-house use by staff. Recent changes in scientific research permits for outside researchers have increased the ability to track specimens that continue to belong to the NPS and often must be accessioned and cataloged offsite at a university or museum (see Issue B on scientific collections). This presents a challenge to the museum program in both coordination and database compatibility and transferability with outside institutions. As part of an ongoing developmental process service-wide, NOCA is seeking to improve its capabilities and streamline the process.

The North Cascades museum collection contains a wide variety of significant collections of archival, historical, archeological, biological and geological collections. A review of the Accession Book and Accession Files found that overall, the park has met NPS standards for accessioning collections for the majority of accessions. Problems remain, however; some can be corrected and others cannot. A summary of observations includes:

- A number of accession file folders are empty, and do not support legal title or accountability requirements. (Ex: NOCA-592, 613-615)

- Some changes in the total number of accessioned materials have been made just through annotations, which do not meet NPS standards. (Ex: NOCA-502, sub-sampling of old magazine collection through marking a black dot next to items to be retained on object list)

- Inadequate description of materials, such as lack of quantities or item counts, or object listings, or descriptions of materials' significance. (Ex: NOCA-611 where newspaper clippings are linked to individuals not named in accession database)

- Almost a total lack of documentation of an appraisal or evaluation process that describes significance, valuation, rarity, or intrinsic value of collections. In one instance appraised values are documented for an incoming loan but no documentation of the source is recorded. (NOCA-507)

Loans to and from North Cascades consist of only a few current active loans coming into the park and one going out. A loan into the park includes some of the collections of the Buckner Homestead and is discussed in Issue E covering the Buckner property. Other loans include the EBLA and SAJH collections. Most loans' materials are up to date but some, such as Buckner, require renewal.

Catalog Records

Cataloging objects and archives produces a specific record of information linked to descriptions and identification of individual items and/or series and groups of items. Once cataloged, museum materials are considered to be fully documented, with exceptions made for items that may justify further research or appraisal. The NOCA curator maintains ANCS+ catalog records for three park units: North Cascades, Ebey's Landing, and San Juan Island, identical to those for accession records.

Table 3 provides a summary of catalog records and item counts currently in the ANCS+ database. Any discrepancies in the total amounts between Table 3 and the Collection Management Report data may be explained, in part, by the information coming from different dates and records that are not yet in the database. Many reasons explain why these two counts exhibit differences. There may be errors, but at this level of review such mistakes cannot easily be detected. After all cataloging is completed and initial estimates are replaced with accurate counts, final reconciliation should be possible. At this time all catalog and accession data are undergoing review.

Some catalog records in the past have been lost (See History of the Museum Collection). Backups are now performed on a regular basis at the park. The park curator needs to work with outside partners and parks to assist with data backup and recovery needs.

DISCIPLINE	NOCA		EBLA		SAJH	
	Total Records	Item Count	Total Records	Item Count	Total Records	Item Count
Archeology	3,621	61,872	1,800	18,190	104,292	374,509
Ethnology	2	2	0	0	0	0
History	1,658	2,922	0	0	269	329
Archival / Manuscript	275	4,917	0	0	785	523.1LF*
Biology	9,994	17,702	0	0	494	1,681
Geology	1203	1303	0	0	28	28
Paleontology	1	1	0	0	39	309
Totals:	16,754	88,719	1,800	18,190	105,907	376,856

Table 3   Total catalog records and item counts for three parks by discipline (as listed by report from ANCS+ database on 8/6/04)   * This number is in linear feet (corresponds to 836,960 pages), and is not included in the sum.

Discussion

The two pillars that any museum program depends upon are proper storage and good recordkeeping. Storage is essential to preservation and protection, and allows physical access to the collections. Recordkeeping is essential for knowing what you have, its source, significance, and history, and allows intellectual access to the information. However, neither of these two essential pillars determines the significance and value of museum object and archive collections. The development of high quality collections is achieved through a professional accessioning process that evaluates potential collections for their suitability for addition to the park's permanent resources.

Accessioning at North Cascades has, for the most part, been performed to service-wide standards. Documentary deficiencies described herein can in most cases be rectified with additions and/or improvements to the records. A thorough comparison of information in the Accession Book, Accession File, and ANCS+ should be performed to ensure accuracy and consistency across these records.

One major needed improvement is documentation of the evaluation criteria and the values and conditions assessments made during the acquisition process. Simply put, in looking at the current accession records, one cannot tell the reasons materials were added to the collection. Was the decision made on the basis of the material's exhibit potential, research value, uniqueness, rarity, link to important themes, places, or individuals? Who recommended the material be accessioned? Who provided an opinion as to its importance or inherent qualities? These attributes need to be documented, as well as the opinions and decisions of park specialists, managers, experts, and private individuals—whoever has provided information and assessments.

The decision to accession materials can be shared and arranged in either formal or informal procedures. One formal technique is the establishment of an accessions committee as described in the *NPS Museum Handbook* Part II. The committee would meet on a regular basis or as needed to evaluate possible additions to the collections, and document the decision-making process. The park may not need a formal committee at this time, given the low volume and lack of complexity of accessions. Nevertheless, the park does need to clarify the steps of the decision-making process and the staff positions involved. The two signatures on the park's Accession Receiving Report should reflect these steps.

Accessioning materials of questionable value has occurred in the past. Examples include published books of recent vintage, magazines, and NPS publications accessioned into the park archives. These items should be classified as library or reference materials, not museum archives (exceptions exist based upon professional appraisals, but they do not apply here). Archives would be addressed during the survey process as described in Issue A.

Other property under discussion for culling includes extensive archeological collections (see Issue B, page 93 and Appendix C, page 101). Buckner Homestead historical items have been discussed as possible landscape features rather than museum artifacts (see Issue E). A variety of historical items of questionable condition or provenance have been observed in the collection, but the extent at this time is unknown without further research and assessment.

It is not feasible to simultaneously evaluate a large and diverse group of materials for de-accessioning. As the park curator is able to group materials for such an evaluation, they can be processed in lots of similar items. An important management consideration is that de-accession of materials known to have been lost, destroyed, or inappropriate to the collection should not be delayed through procrastination and sloth—museum collections are expensive to store, document, and preserve. The park has limited space and staff time to care for its valuable collections. Inappropriate materials and those beyond recovery (decay is too advanced to justify treatment) take their toll in real costs to the NPS. Progress on this goal should be an annual accomplishment work goal, with support from the Regional Office CRM staff.

The park has made progress on cataloging its backlog. NOCA's *Collection Management Report* (2003) shows some 27,400 items in its backlog which is approximately 20% of its total collection count. This year's work by the NOCA curator includes the following catalog records recorded in ANCS+:

NOCA Cultural	2,055
NOCA Natural	150
SAJH Cultural	23
SAJH Natural	19
EBLA Cultural	800

The number of the total objects cataloged is a moving target. As new materials are accessioned and then cataloged, the percentage may shift higher or lower. The objective is to completely document the collections. While this is rarely achieved in practice, without continual effort the amount of backlog can grow substantially. For this reason, the NPS has a policy that all projects that generate collections budget for their curation and data entry.

A review of older catalog records shows that primarily the cultural resource records would benefit from updating. The natural history records need little in the way of updating, largely as a result of the systematic manner in which biologists record field data. However, given the effort to catalog backlog and the large number of older records, most parks recognize their inability to make headway in updating until such time as new service-wide updates are funded on a project basis. Still, the curator can and should make occasional updates as time and attention allow. (See discussion in Issue F on planning, programming, and staffing).

The park curator is taking adequate steps to ensure that electronic records are backed up electronically on a regular basis. The park can and should develop standards for parks and partners to create and/or maintain ANCS+ records backups that are delivered to the NOCA curator for inspection and protection.

Both Ebey's Landing and San Juan Island have letters of agreement signed in 2004 that delineate responsibilities for curation and storage of collections at the Marblemount facility. These letters establish the NOCA curator position as curator-of-record serving the other two parks. NOCA should develop standard operating procedures that describe how approval and processing of accessions will occur, the access to and maintenance of ANCS+ database, and backup and security procedures. The need for changes from current practices is not anticipated, but a written SOP will help managers and staff understand roles and functions, and orient and educate new staff.

Recommendations

- Complete accession records to the fullest extent possible. Ensure that every accession has an Accession Receiving Report and List of Objects. Renew loans that have passed their expiration date.

- Develop an acquisition evaluation process that includes documenting the reasons that materials have been accepted into the collection. Delineate signature authorities and the decision-making process.

- De-accession inappropriate objects and archives as soon as possible. Procrastination has a real and substantial cost.

- Complete backlog cataloging, using project funds where necessary.

- Re-catalog materials where needed. Incremental changes may be made when items are handled or studied for other purposes. Larger projects will require additional staff or funding.

- Continue backing up ANCS+ databases. Work with parks and partners to establish data security standards.

- Develop standard operating procedures for recordkeeping across the three parks for which records are maintained by the NOCA curator.

Figure 5   Buckner Homestead farm vehicle

Issue Statement

A comprehensive plan is required for the preservation and management of cultural resources at this site.

Background

Acquired by the National Park Service in 1970, the Buckner Homestead Historic District is located at the head of Lake Chelan in the Lake Chelan National Recreation Area (LACH) of the North Cascades National Park Service Complex (NOCA). Listed on the National Register of Historic Places, the Homestead is a locally significant cultural resource. It constitutes a physical record of the development of the entrepreneurial farming, mining, timber, and trapping industries that laid the foundations characteristic of rural mountain communities and economies of the interior Pacific Northwest. The 90-acre district includes over 200 apple trees, hay fields, pastures, about 50 pieces of farm equipment, hundreds of artifacts, and many buildings and structures built over the past 100 years.

While originally homesteaded by Bill Buzzard, the indelible character of the present homestead was determined by 70 subsequent years of work and play by the Buckner family. During that time the homestead was constantly evolving in innovative ways to remain in commercial operation; no single period of its existence best characterizes the resource. No longer functioning as a commercial homestead/orchard, the resource continues as a constantly evolving interpretive site, a community gathering place, and a park employee housing unit. Consequently, preservation is a challenge, especially when isolation, environment, and lack of staff and funds are factored into the program as well.

Over the years a number of documents and plans have been completed for NOCA and include mention of the Buckner Homestead. Relevant documents are included in the park reference section of the bibliography.

The NOCA museum collection currently has five accessions related to the Buckner Homestead. This section will discuss only two—the materials actually acquired when the park purchased the Weaver property (LACH-00001, NOCA-00502), and the 45 items loaned by the Buckner sisters in 1988 (LACH-00012, NOCA-00507). Museum collections have specific preservation requirements that are currently not possible at the Buckner Homestead. Presently many artifacts in these accessions are located outside in the landscape, with only a few exceptions located inside historic structures.

As documented by photographs taken ca 1987-1988 and 2003, the objects have drastically deteriorated despite conservation work on several items and construction of shed roofs over others. In fact, the shed roofs have exacerbated the problem in at least one case by collapsing under an abnormally heavy snowfall and crushing the object it was protecting. The workshop has many objects remaining from the homestead days which are not accessioned. In addition, the NPS has moved maintenance tools and equipment and interpretive objects into it. This space is open for the visitor to discover, and the co-mingling of possible historic artifacts with contemporary tools adds no value to the historic site.

The *Buckner Homestead Historic District Final Management Plan* outlined the processes for identifying the objects to be permanently acquired from the Buckner sisters, and for their long-term preservation and interpretation. But this part of the plan has not been implemented. The park has not identified these objects and has not implemented a conservation and maintenance plan for their care. The parts of the plan that have been implemented are related to the historic structures and the orchard.

The park is currently investing about $30,000 to $35,000 per year from a combination of ONPS funding and NPS Cultural Cyclic Maintenance funding to manage the apple orchard. The management of the orchard is done by a term horticulturist who works about nine or ten months per year. The park curator is only able to spend about two weeks per year dealing with all the issues at Stehekin, including the items currently identified as museum objects located at the Homestead.

Under the auspices of Washington's National Park Fund, the Buckner Homestead Heritage Foundation was established to fundraise for special projects at the Buckner Homestead. This group is comprised of members of the Buckner family, the Stehekin community, and non-voting NPS liaisons. They have raised funds for the reconstruction of the apple packing shed.

Discussion

Although the park has an approved plan for the Buckner Homestead, *Buckner Homestead Historic District Final Management Plan*, only the rehabilitation of the apple orchard and irrigation system, and maintenance of the historic structures has been implemented. One possible reason for the failure of previous preservation efforts and resulting deterioration of cultural resources has been the lack of consistent and adequate staffing and funding to implement that plan. Planning and management efforts have been conceived, funded, and implemented for the most part by single divisions or branches of park staff, rather than the park as a whole.

As part of the in-briefing for this Museum Management Plan, the superintendent asked the MMP team if they would comment on the appropriateness of efforts to preserve the historic orchard. The MMP team did not feel qualified to address the orchard in isolation. However, the following discussion and recommendations will attempt to provide that guidance from a cultural resource and collection management perspective for the Buckner Homestead in total.

The museum management program at the park has been attempting to maintain collections as "museum property." The park will not be able to provide even the basic levels of security and preservation required for the management of museum collections at the site of the Buckner Homestead. Even if the park had the required funding and staff, the necessary structures and technology would alter the site so as to destroy its value as a historic district and cultural landscape.

Without this intervention, the objects at the site will continue to deteriorate, will continue to disappear by theft, and will continue to be moved from place to place, thus continuing to alter the historic appearance of the site.

It is possible to maintain the historic structures at the site, mostly through the application of specific funding sources, such as Cultural Cyclic Maintenance. Cultural Cyclic Maintenance funds may also be used for the preservation maintenance of large machinery items, and this option could be extended to cover much of the material at the site. Documentation and recording of these resources is required, followed by a schedule for preservation treatment.

In order to preserve the buildings and the landscape, the 1998 management plan must be updated. A Cultural Landscape Report (CLR) is needed to complete the documentation and establish a treatment plan for the area as a whole. A grid-applied documentation of the machinery and tools at the Homestead should be central to the CLR, and include treatment plans for these major items and concentrations of smaller materials.

This is a slightly different application of the Cultural Landscape Report approach, and will require the addition of specialists not generally associated with this effort. In addition to the cultural landscape architect, the following specialists should be included: an historical archeologist to assist with the mapping and documentation of materials; an historical architect to address the historic structures; an historical agricultural curator to assist with identification of specialized machinery, tools and work areas; a conservator to suggest long term preservation methodologies; and an historic orchard specialist. A health and safety specialist should be included to address those concerns as well. The various natural resource and interpretive specialists working at the park also need to be consulted, and information concerning their various projects related to this district should be included in the CLR. Last but not least, the Buckner family and other representatives of the Stehekin community should be consulted.

The end product of such an effort would be both a full documentation of all the associated parts of the resource, and a series of interlocking plans for the maintenance and preservation of the Buckner Homestead as a whole. Not only would such an effort address the preservation needs, but would concentrate all known information concerning this resource in one document. This would have obvious benefits for both management and interpretation efforts.

In order to complete the CLR, a PMIS project statement should be completed. The cultural landscape program staff in the Pacific West Regional Office can provide assistance in drafting the statement as well as in estimating the total cost. The Cultural Resource Preservation Program (CRPP) Base requests for FY 2006 will be prioritized in February 2005. Although the park has prioritized a number of projects for the next five years for CRPP Base, the need for action on the Buckner Homestead would suggest that this request might be pushed to the top of the list. The combined call will be coming out soon; a new PMIS project statement should be prepared and proposed for FY 2006 funding.

In the interim, ongoing maintenance should be continued. A plan to remove vegetation from around objects to reduce the continued deterioration should be developed. This would also allow the objects to dry out during the summer, which will assist in some additional preservation. The objects that are currently listed as museum property should be de-accessioned and then managed as park property. The items in the workshop should be evaluated to identify those that should be placed in the park collection, in storage, or on display in park museum exhibits. The remainder should be removed from the park, and the building used for park maintenance activities and closed to the public.

Conclusion

A strict museum approach to the preservation and management of resources at the Buckner Homestead is impossible due to the condition of the objects, lack of funding and staff, and the factors of distance, environment, National Register status, and working nature of the current operations. Other cultural resource management and interpretative approaches have failed for the same reason. Since it is not possible to apply museum standards to the management of these resources on site, continued efforts in this manner are wasteful and counterproductive.

The park should build on the current documentation that is in place, and develop a holistic approach to the management of these resources. The best way to do that would be through a Cultural Landscape Report and associated treatment plans created by a group of specialists using the methodologies of their varied disciplines. In this manner all the needs of the Buckner Homestead will be considered jointly, and treatments can be applied that will benefit the preservation of the total resource rather than isolated segments.

Recommendations

- Complete a PMIS statement to be funded out of CRPP Base for FY 2007 for a Cultural Landscape Report for the Buckner Homestead that will address the full range of preservation concerns.

- Provide maintenance to the site and artifacts until the CLR is completed by continuation of current practices and by removal of vegetation around objects in order to slow the deterioration.

- Update the loan agreement with Buckner family but manage the objects as park property rather than museum collections.

- Arrange for donation of the items identified in the plan and for removal of those not when the CLR has been completed and approved.

- De-accession those cataloged items that are at the site and transfer those that are remaining to park property records.

Issue Statement

Management of the museum object and archive collections requires an integrated approach by trained and professional staff to plan, budget, and implement successful programs that support park operations.

Background

North Cascades National Park Service Complex has a museum collection of about 170,000 items. From the beginning of the park until 1988, the museum collection was managed by collateral duty staff with occasional temporary museum technicians under the Division of Interpretation. In that year the management of the collection was assumed by the Resource Management Division. As a result of the 1994 *Collection Management Plan* and the NPS reorganization, in 1995 the park created a branch of cultural resources under the Resource Management Division. Two Pacific Northwest Region employees assigned to North Cascades were transferred to the park and a permanent subject-to-furlough museum technician position was created. This position is now a GS-1015-11 museum curator and currently subject-to-furlough with only 13 pay periods of funding available from NOCA base.

In FY 2004 the NOCA base budget is $5,785,900, of which about 23% or $1,256,700 is established for Resource Management. These figures include the Cultural Resources Branch: $191,175 for 2.46 FTE, reflecting the natural resource priority in a park created for wilderness values. The growth of natural collections and field records because of the recent emphasis on inventory and monitoring has increased the workload for the curator.

In 1995 the NOCA curator became the curator-of-record for San Juan Island National Historical Park (SAJH) and in 2004 for Ebey's Landing National Historical Reserve (EBLA). The archeological collections from these parks are stored at the NOCA Marblemount facility. In addition, the Burke Museum at the University of Washington has a large prehistoric archeological collection from SAJH. The NOCA curator provides oversight and contact on these items with the Burke Museum archeology section staff. In FY 2004 SAJH provided $13,000 in base funds for museum management while EBLA provided $1600. The remainder of the NOCA curator's funding comes from a variety of project funds including Backlog Cataloging, Museum Collections Preservation and Protection Program, archeology projects, and various natural resource project funds from all three parks. In FY 2004 the curator has managed to find funding for the entire fiscal year; however, this searching for funds takes time away from museum work and can be demoralizing.

These funds provide for individual projects to be completed. But they do not allow the park to expand the museum management program to adequately address the needs of both park staff and the public for access, or for the on-going preservation and protection of the museum and archival collections. At the present time the museum curator is permanent subject-to-furlough. There are no Operations Formulation System (OFS) requests for a base increase for the museum management program for NOCA.

San Juan Island National Historical Park has a museum object and archive collection of over one million items, primarily archeological. Two-thirds of the objects are located at the Burke Museum. But the Marblemount facility at NOCA houses one-third of the material and the NOCA curator manages the collections and all the recordkeeping. As noted above, in FY 2004 SAJH provided $13,000 in base funds and additional project funds of $10,000 from the Backlog Catalog program. When the agreement between NOCA and SAJH was first initiated, the agreement was for SAJH to provide $10,000 per year. At that time the funds paid for half the year of the park curator (due to lower grade). However, in the ten years since then, costs have gone up significantly but the amount that SAJH has been able to provide has not kept pace. SAJH does have an Operations Formulation System (OFS) request (10622A: Multi-park request: Meet Curatorial Needs for SAJH/NOCA) at priority four to increase the funding for the museum program. If received, this funding would convert the NOCA curator to full time, hire a subject-to-furlough museum technician, and provide support funds for supplies, travel, and professional development.

At Ebey's Landing National Historical Reserve, initial planning provided for NPS to own very little land in the reserve and accomplishing programs through partnerships. As a partnership park unit, the reserve was not expected to collect museum objects and archive collections. However, a series of events in the late 1990s and early 2000s led to the purchase and donation of several pieces of property which included historic structures in need of stabilization. As part of this work, archeological excavations were required and an archeological collection was created. These materials are located at the Marblemount facility at NOCA.

The North Coast and Cascades Network has a number of journeyman-level curators. As the network management grows, these professional staff can support each other and provide differing strengths. The network does not have, however, an archivist (GS-1420-11). Archival collections are the fastest growing collections in the National Park Service and, in some cases, provide the only documentation of research that is happening or has happened in the parks. The need for follow-up on the research and collecting permits that have been issued for the parks is also growing. A partnership with the network data managers is a critical need for the museum program, and a museum technician (GS-1016-07) would provide that support.

Discussion

The museum program crosses many disciplines and subject areas. North Cascades National Park, Ebey's Landing National Historical Reserve, San Juan Island National Historical Park, and the North Coast and Cascades Network must continue to take an aggressive approach to long-range planning for the effective development of the museum management program's budget, and staff necessary to preserve its resources and complete its missions. A proactive approach to necessary planning and programming will allow the staff to complete work that will help preserve park resources and educate the public.

It is important to maintain perspective and to determine how resource management activities support the overall missions and goals of the park in planning for all resource preservation. The resources that make up the museum object and archive collections constitute documentary evidence of park resource management activities and the administrative decisions affecting them. Park museum collections *are* primary resources and comprise the park's institutional memory. From the perspective of this planning team, the museum management program should serve four distinct functions within the park: documentation; preservation; research; and education and public programs.

The museum curator has the primary responsibility for producing the planning, programming, and reporting necessary to ensure that the primary functions mentioned above are adequately staffed, funded, and performed. To achieve this goal, the interrelationships of the various reporting and planning documents must be considered. These include the Collection Management Report (CMR), the Checklist for the Preservation and Protection of Museum Collections (Checklist), the Resource Management Plan (RMP), the Project Management Information System (PMIS), Operations Formulation Systems (OFS), and various program-specific documents. By understanding these relationships, the curator can produce effective programming documents that will secure funding from available sources. Although the *Museum Handbook*, Parts I, II, and III, provide overall guidance for the NPS museum program, the museum staff needs to bring their professional expertise to addressing the needs of museum collections.

The documentation of time and costs to the museum management program for individual elements of the four primary functions mentioned above is an essential element of planning and programming. Increasingly, park managers are asked to show "value received for value given" in their operations. The response "to comply with regulations" is often not sufficient justification for funding in today's climate of lean budgets and reduced staff. Sometimes it is difficult for the non-specialist reviewing budget requests to perceive exactly what the "value received" to the park actually is, so illustrations of "value" in planning documents, budget requests, and reports must be overt and proactive.

The park curator and the chief of the Cultural Resources Branch should complete a cost analysis for both the current and projected activities of the branch as a means to establish credibility for the management of park museum collections. Some very basic time and cost analysis questions might include:

- How many accessions have been processed over the past three years?

- Is the rate of new accessions entering the collections increasing or decreasing?

- Is the park keeping up with basic registration, or is a backlog being created?

- What is the average time/cost to process an accession?

- What is the average time/cost to catalog an object?

- What is the time/cost to provide Integrated Pest Management (IPM), preventive maintenance, and environmental monitoring per year?

- What is the time/cost to provide storage/inventory per cubic foot of storage per year?

- How many requests for research access to the collections are received each year from both staff and public, and what is the time/cost per request to provide that access?

- Have the requests for access increased or decreased over the past three years?

- Have collections and/or documentation been used for educational purposes?

After the staff collects, analyzes, and formats these types of data for preservation, park management will begin to recognize the direct costs associated with various facets of collection management and to determine whether essential work is being accomplished in a timely manner. With these data, park staff will be able to develop effective, integrated programs to identify, program for, and meet park needs. The data will also document where project or temporary staff may be necessary to accomplish backlogged work or to make the overall program more efficient. Finally, this information will provide the foundation and documentation for establishing appropriate staffing levels, both in numbers of positions and grade levels.

The parks should seek additional funding sources for curatorial projects to provide needed assistance in cataloging and museum collection management. The parks' cooperating association, Northwest Interpretive Association (NWIA), Washington's National Parks Fund, and local foundation offices should be approached with specific project requests tailored to organizational interests.

A number of graduate programs, including a museum program at the University of Washington, may provide interns to do professional level museum project work under the direction of other museum professionals. The American Association of Museums has a list of such accredited programs. The NPS has a cooperative agreement with the National Council for Preservation Education that provides a clearinghouse for interns from appropriate college and university programs for parks. Finally, the American Institute for Conservation has a list of conservation programs.

If free housing could be found, perhaps free or nearly free interns with professional training to work on specific projects at the park could also be found. Stipends can be funded with project money or even through support from the PNIA. The Pacific West Region museum management staff, the Museum Management Program in WASO, the Western Archeological and Conservation Center (WACC), and the Division of Conservation at Harpers Ferry Center may provide assistance, recommendations, and additional oversight, if needed.

As an essential part of park operations, the museum management program should have a separate ONPS budget in addition to project funds. This will allow program identification and tracking of funds required and spent for the preservation of park-specific resources. If the network-based museum management program is carried out, appropriate levels of increased base funding could be managed by the network in collaboration with the three parks' chiefs of resources management.

Once project(s) are completed to deal with the backlog need (as documented throughout this plan), the NOCA Museum Management Program does not appear to need a full-time archivist (GS-1420-11) on-site but could rely upon the services of a network archivist (which might be located at NOCA). Perhaps the parks could explore using natural resource funds to assist with the museum technician (GS-1016-07) position, which could also assume the permit function for the parks. This would allow the science advisor currently involved in permitting issues greater time for project work. Such a strategy would undoubtedly also help to ensure that natural resources collections issues are addressed during planning and programming for research projects.

The park might also investigate partnership opportunities with other federal agencies (U.S. Forest Service, Bureau of Land Management), local and regional agencies, or non-governmental agencies. As the management of public lands moves further towards management of ecosystems rather than by the artificial political boundaries, it becomes more efficient for all concerned to manage resources in a more holistic manner. This would also make it easier for outside researchers who could do "one-stop-shopping" rather than having to go to a number of different locations.

The parks are in various stages of planning. EBLA and SAJH are in the General Management Plan (GMP) process. NOCA has a GMP for North Cascades National Park, Ross Lake National Recreation Area, and Lake Chelan National Recreation (1988), and a separate Lake Chelan *Final General Management Plan and Environmental Impact Statement* (1995). The museum management program is not adequately addressed in either NOCA plan but the curator has been participating in the planning for SAJH.

NOCA does not have a Long Range Interpretive Plan (LRIP) although one has been begun by park staff. The current *Interpretive Prospectus* (1990) is considered very out of date. A coherent program of use of the museum collection in exhibits is not identified in the plan. The Cultural Resources Branch and the park curator have not been participating in the planning for the LRIP. In order to integrate the museum management program into the interpretive program, it is important for them to be a part of the planning effort. No LRIP is available for EBLA.

The NOCA *Resource Management Plan* (RMP) was last updated in 1999 and contains a number of project statements related to the museum program; these are reflected in the park's PMIS program. However, the narrative does not provide a roadmap for managing these important resources but rather a history of what has occurred.

The entire SAJH RMP (c. 1993) was not available for review but one project statement was provided. EBLA has an RMP that was approved in 1995 and updated in 1999. It has not been updated since 1999 because the software hasn't been available. Once new RMP guidance is received, the museum management program should be an integral part of the narrative plan as well as the programming documents that support that plan.

As the museum management program is organizationally located in the Resources Management Division, it is in a unique position to ensure that natural resources collections are addressed during planning and programming. This includes the projects that will be on-going in the inventory and monitoring program as well as those in network programs. In addition, the Cultural Resources Branch includes the park archeologist. Planning for archeological projects must from their beginning consider the cataloging, storage, and conservation of collections. These issues are discussed in greater depth in Issue B.

Currently, the parks have a number of statements for museum needs in PMIS but they do not truly comprise a coherent five-year outline for the combined museum management program for each park. This plan provides some guidance for such a program.

Two other critical reporting documents provide data for managing the park's museum collections as well as identifying funding needs: the Checklist for Preservation and Protection of Museum Collections and the Collection Management Report (CMR).

The Checklist for Preservation and Protection of Museum Collections (Checklist) is an important document from several different viewpoints:

- It establishes the standards under which park museum collections are maintained and against which the park evaluates it.

- It documents the preservation of the park museum collections at a particular point in time.

- It determines the funding needed to bring a museum collection to standard.

The Checklist is divided by facility and type, i.e., a structure that holds both exhibit and storage would have two checklists. The park must complete and/or update this document on an annual basis. The Museum Collection Preservation and Protection Program (MCPPP) funding is based on the data received from park Checklists. Thus, their careful completion is critical to adequately estimate the needs of the parks. The service-wide funding is divided by a formula based on total needs for each of the seven NPS regions. Every four years this funding is adjusted based on the most current data so the data must be accurately reflective of present needs.

The Collection Management Report provides a statistical overview of the park's present collection. It provides park staff and management, as well as the region and the service-wide programs with information on size and type of collection; the growth of the collection over time; documentation of use; and identification of uncataloged backlog. This latter is critical as it relates to funding. The service-wide Backlog Catalog Program fund distribution is based on this report so it must accurately reflect the total park collection, especially with regard to the uncataloged backlog. As noted for MCPPP, reallocation and distribution of these funds is based on the backlog reported on the CMR.

Although all three parks report a backlog on their 2003 CMRs, the MMP team noted a backlog of materials, especially archives, which is not accessioned and thus not reported in the backlog. Until these materials are accessioned, the parks do not have an accurate record of its backlog and is unable to receive funds to process and catalog these materials. All museum and archival materials that have been identified as belonging to the parks' collections must be accessioned by the end of each fiscal year. The numbers can be estimates and later refined during the processing and cataloging of the materials. Other sections of this plan provide more guidance on this subject.

Recommendations

- Update the SAJH OFS (10622A) or draft a new request, working with the North Coast and Cascades Network, to establish a fulltime curator to manage the collections for EBLA, NOCA, and SAJH. This request should include an archivist (GS-1420-11) and a museum technician (GS-1016-07) to provide guidance and support for the museum object and archive collections of the network, as well as support funds for supplies, travel, and professional development.

- Revise the parks' PMIS statements. Add new project statements that accurately define current needs in archives and museum management for the parks. These project statements taken as a whole should define a five-year program for the parks' museum management program.

- Revise the Checklists based on the recommendations of this MMP.

- Accession all backlog collections to ensure that the parks are eligible to receive Backlog Cataloging funds.

- Revise the resource management and other plans as opportunities arise, and participate in interpretive planning to address the specific needs of the museum management program.

Suggested Standard Operating Procedure

The purpose of this SOP is to aid park staff in accomplishing their responsibilities according to DO#77 (*Natural Resources Management Guideline*), DO#28 (*Cultural Resources Management Guideline*), DM 411 (*DOI Property Management Regulations*), DO#19 (*Records Management Guideline*), 36 CFR 2.9, and legislation associated with archiving resource management records.

The *Museum Management Plan* (2004) documents the need for guidelines on the management of archival material. Recommendations include retention of reports of archeological, historical, architectural, and other scientific research conducted within and for the park.

The parks' archives include many unique information resources that need professional organization and arrangement to promote their most efficient use. Park resource management staffs generate records on a daily basis that should be considered for inclusion in the park archives. Staff is creating data sets, photographs, maps, and field notebooks that future generations will need to access to research the history of cultural and natural resource projects at the parks.

Park staffs are involved in capturing fire monitoring data, plant collections, air quality research, and a host of ethnographic and archeological research. Preserving the corporate knowledge of each of these individual activities depends ultimately upon the archival process. The organizing thread, then, should be the project itself.

Archeological Records

Government-wide regulations for the curation and care of federal archeological collections required by the National Historic Preservation Act (NHPA), the Reservoir Salvage Act, and the Archeological Resources Protection Act (ARPA) were issued in 1990 as "Curation of Federally Owned and Administered Archaeological Collections" (36 CFR 79). These regulations establish procedures and guidelines to manage and preserve collections. They also include terms and conditions for federal agencies to include in contracts and cooperative agreements with non-federal repositories.

The document 36 CFR 79 covers excavations done under the authority or in connection with federal agencies, laws, and permits (Antiquities Act, Reservoir Salvage Act, Section 110 of NHPA, ARPA). It also applies to the collections and the generated data, or associated records and is applicable to both new and preexisting collections

Associated records are defined as "Original records (or copies thereof) that are prepared, assembled and document efforts to locate, evaluate, record, study, preserve or recover a prehistoric or historic resource. Some records such as field notes, artifact inventories, and oral histories may be originals that are prepared as a result of the fieldwork, analysis and report preparation. Other records such as deeds, survey plats, historical maps, and diaries may be copies of original public or archival documents that are assembled and studied as a result of historical research (36 CFR Part 79.4.a.2)."

These guidelines are provided so future materials can be processed and included in the collection in a systematic fashion. Staff may also use this procedure for materials already in their possession in preparation for the materials being accessioned or registered by the archivist under the park museum collection accountability system, the National Park Service Automated National Cataloging System (ANCS+). Accessioning is the preliminary step in identifying collections that will later be cataloged and processed to NPS archival standards. Eventually, finding aids are created to enable staff and researchers to easily access information in the collection archives.

Staff cooperation in carrying out this SOP will greatly accelerate the rate at which materials are processed. Subject matter specialists involved in the creation of these materials carry the greater knowledge about these collections. The quality of the final product will depend upon the quality of staff involvement in the process of identifying the exact nature of archival materials.

Checklist for Preparing Field Documentation

1) Obtain an accession number from the park curator at the commencement of all new field projects.

2) Label ALL materials with the project accession number. Use a soft lead pencil for marking documents or files and a Mylar marking pen for Mylar enclosures such as slide, print or negative sleeves.

3) Materials must be arranged by material type such as field notes, reports, maps, correspondence, photographs, etc. Each group of materials should be stored in individual folders or acceptable archival enclosures.

4) Resource management staff is responsible for turning over all project documentation to the park curator upon completion of a project. In the interest of preserving institutional knowledge, leave collections in their original order. Original order means the organization system created by the originator of a document collection. RESIST the urge to take important documents from these collections. If something is needed for future use, copy it or request that the curator make a copy. After copying, replace the document or photo where it was found. MUCH INFORMATION ABOUT PAST PROJECTS HAS BEEN LOST BECAUSE COLLECTIONS HAVE BEEN PICKED APART. REMEMBER THESE MATERIALS WILL ALWAYS BE AVAILABLE. That is the whole point behind establishing archives.

5) When the archival documentation is transferred to the park museum, the form below should be provided. This form includes the project title, principal investigator, date of project and a history of the project. The name of the individual who obtained the accession number should also be listed. The type and quantity of documentation would be included as well, such as maps (13), field notes (4 notebooks), Correspondence (3 files).

USE ONE COPY OF THE ATTACHED Project Identification Sheet FOR EACH PROJECT.

Project Identification Sheet

Accession No: _____(Assigned only by Curator)

Your name, title, office: _____

Project Title_____

_____

Principle Investigator and position at NEPE during project. Please list staff who might have aided in the project implementation.

_____

_____

_____

Researcher's office location and extension, or current address, occupation, and employer or contact number.

_____

_____

_____

Type and quantity of materials in collection(s) (specimens, papers, files, reports, data, maps, photo prints/negatives/slides, computer media - format/software?) Condition. (i.e. infested, torn, broken, good) Attach additional paper if necessary.

_____

_____

_____

Scope of Project:

Is this collection part of an ongoing project to be updated annually? Yes _____ No_____
Research goals or project purpose and published or in-house reports to which collection relates

_____

_____

_____

Abstract of collection content. Keywords referring to geographical locations, processes, data types, associated projects. Indicate whether specimens/objects were collected. Attach additional paper if necessary.

_____

_____

_____

Planning for the Curation of Resource Management Records

Records in the Field

Anticipate the kinds of documents that will be needed in the field to record data and use archival materials to produce them (e.g., field excavation forms, field notes, photographic logs, transit data, maps, level records, and videotape). Use archival quality materials in the field. This can reduce the cost of copying information onto archival quality media later. Remember that documentation on electronic media alone is not sufficient because of the lack of long-term stability of these media and their contents.

The records created in the field, as well as in the lab, are vulnerable to insects, vermin, mold, humidity, light, temperature changes, and mishandling. They are also vulnerable to a variety of environmental threats, such as roof leaks, flooding, fire, and asbestos problems, and to theft or other malicious action. The following are a number of general recommendations to follow in the field and lab in order to promote the long-term preservation and viability of the great variety of records created:

- Use appropriate long-lived media for all record types.

- Use permanent and archival stock in paper, ink, lead pencil, folders, and boxes.

- Inspect and redo damaged or inadequate records.

- Label everything, or their containers.

- Use appropriate storage for all media in the field in order to protect them from poor environmental conditions and threat of fire or theft.

- Carefully consider existing guidelines and equipment for digital and audiovisual media, make sure backup copies and hard copy printouts exist, and migrate data to updated software on a regular schedule.

- Ensure that project information and data is captured by appropriately knowledgeable staff.

Paper records

A number of conservation principles should also be considered for each of the primary types of media used for associated records.

- Use high alpha cellulose, lignin free, acid-free paper, especially for field notebooks, and standardized forms.

- Record information using archival (permanent carbon) inks or #4 (HH) pencils.

- Protect paper from water and humidity, and minimize its exposure to light.

- Try not to fold or roll paper.

- Store papers in archival folders in polyethylene boxes.

Photographs

- Protect all photographic materials (e.g., film, prints, slides, negatives, and transparencies) from heat, rain, and wind. Store them in archival folders in polyethylene boxes.

- Maintain a log of all photographic images.

- Only handle photos along their edges. Do not touch the image with bare fingers.

- Do not use paper or plastic clips, rubber bands, pressure sensitive tape, adhesive or pressure sensitive labels, or Post-it® notes directly on photographs.

- Do not put photographic materials, except unused film, in cold storage without reformatting them for access and duplication.

Magnetic Records

- Protect all magnetic materials (e.g., audio tapes, video tapes) from heat, dust, and dirt.

- Consider the equipment required to play the audiovisual material and the longevity of that equipment.

- Label all records in a permanent, carbon-based ink.

- Store the records in their cases in polyethylene boxes.

Cartographic and Oversized Records

- Oversized records should be stored flat in folders, preferably in map cases. Do not roll or fold.

- Protect paper from water and minimize its exposure to light.

- During storage and use, protect oversized records from tears and rips. Do not use tape to repair tears.

- Label the oversized folders in permanent, carbon-based ink.

Digital Records and Data

- Produce your master records in uncompressed TIFF format, if possible. Avoid using proprietary file formats or lossy compression.

- Protect all digital records from heat, dust, dirt, and ultraviolet radiation.

- Choose a storage medium that is considered a standard. Research its longevity.

- Keep digital records away from magnetic or electric fields that are created by old telephones, static, and field and lab equipment such as magnetometers and 12-volt transformers. Computer diskettes can be partially or completely erased by such exposure.

- Label the records in permanent, carbon-based ink.

Appendix B— Preparing Inactive Records for Transfer to Storage

The records management program is able to assist park divisions, branches, and offices to professionally and legally manage the records created and received in the course of performing the park's business. This program can provide legal and technical advice regarding the management of records in offices as well as in park retention storage locations housing inactive records. Retention periods for National Park Service records are specified either in the General Records Schedule (GRS), the Federal Government's guideline on retention/disposition of records common to all government agencies, and NPS-19, *Records Management Guideline*, Appendix B, Records Retention Schedule.

It is the responsibility of each park office wishing to retire inactive records to fully prepare them to the specifications that follow before they may be transferred to the park museum collection. Once this is done, the park curator or his/her representative will visit the office to verify the preparation and physically transfer the records to the museum collection. Of course, park museum staff will be happy to provide assistance in the interpretation of these instructions at any time during the preparation of records for transfer.

- No records are to be dropped off at the curator's office without full prior preparation and approval of the Curator.
- Records received unannounced or unprepared will be returned to the owning office.

ALL files pertaining to agency business are government property, not the property of the individual employee.

Preparing Records for Transfer

- Use only approved GSA Records Storage Boxes, NSN 8115-00-117-8249, or approved archival boxes. These boxes can be ordered through GSA for large quantities of records, or the park museum may be able to provide boxes if only a few are required.

- Remove all files from hanging folders and three-ring binders. Place in appropriately sized (legal or letter) folders that fully contain the records without folding. Any file exceeding one inch in thickness, such as thick files contained in binders, must be split between multiple folders (place in two or more folders). This rule does not apply to Contracting Project files, which are self-contained packages and may be thicker. Number multiple folders "F1/2, F2/2", etc.

- Make certain EVERY folder has a clear label, typed or neatly handwritten, indicating a clear, descriptive title of the contents, the date or date range of the file and, preferably, a file code and retention period. NPS file codes are not mandatory, but they make records review and disposition actions must faster and simpler and provide a common scheme for filing of related documents. File codes are not necessarily appropriate for project files as they may contain a large variety of materials that do not fit within a file code.

- Remove all personal materials and multiple copies of documents (keep no more than two). Remove all blank forms.

- Remove all office supplies and computer materials such as desk supplies, computer manuals, miscellaneous diskettes, etc.

- Consult with Records Management staff for assistance with odd-size and unusual format materials such as engineering drawings, photographs, audio and videotapes, etc. Do not combine these materials in boxes with standard-sized records in folders, unless they are an integral part of a particular file. NEVER fold oversize materials to fit into record storage boxes.

Electronic Records

Many word-processed and other types of documents are now received in electronic format and are used that way in park offices. The preservation of records in electronic format is a very problematic issue, one which much larger agencies are having difficulty grappling with. The park curator advises all park departments that preserving records in electronic format is not possible at this time, as neither the hardware nor software capability to do so is available.

Make sure to print hard copy of critical and important records and interfile them with the related paper records. Hard copy records have a proven history of preservation capability. The curator will be happy to discuss the management of databases in electronic form for long-term storage and preservation. All electronic mail and word processing documents that must be retained for either temporary legal purposes or are permanently valuable as archival materials MUST be printed and transferred to records storage in hard copy format.

Records Series and Records Disposition

In archives and records management terminology, records are dealt with in groupings called "series." A series is a group of records which may be defined either by format or conditions of creation or use. A more formal definition may be "file units or documents arranged according to a filing system or kept together because they relate to a particular subject or function, result from the same activity, document a specific kind of transaction, take a particular physical form, or have some other relationship arising out of their creation, receipt, or use, such as restrictions on access and use." A records series is generally handled as a unit for disposition purposes.[1]

Examples of series in National Park Service records include: contract project files; time and attendance records; alphabetical subject files; purchase orders; and press releases. Records are handled in series because these categories may be designated within the National Park Service Records Disposition Schedule for authorized legal periods of retention. Some series (such as budget, human resources, and contracting) records may be destroyed after keeping for a certain period for legal purposes. Other types of records, generally all records dealing with management of resources and

---

[1] Definitions provided in this paragraph are taken from Appendix D: Glossary, Disposition of Federal Records: A Records Management Handbook, Washington, DC: National Archives and Records Administration, 1992.

administrative decision process, etc., have permanent value and are retained as archives collections. For this reason, the museum staff asks that records be managed and retired in identifiable series to increase the ease of handling when assigning retention periods and, later, in destroying or transferring records to appropriate locations.

"Disposition" in records management is defined as "the actions taken regarding records no longer needed for current government business." These actions can include transfer to storage facilities, destruction, or transfer to archives. In this instance, "disposition" does not automatically mean destruction.

Packing Records for Transfer

Try to place only one record series with one disposition date in a box. Records will later be disposed of by box, not by removing individual files from boxes. *Example:* Place all retiring DI-1s in a group of boxes. This is one 'series' of records, all one document type with all the same destruction date. If a single series doesn't fill a box, different series may be combined in a box for space economy, as long as they are clearly labeled.

Pack the files in the same sequence in the cartons as they are arranged in the file drawer, using the same filing system as that used in the office. Place folders with labels facing the front of the box (label area), or facing to the right of front if the folders are legal sized.

Do not over pack boxes. One must be able to slip a hand easily between folders and get into the hand-holds. If this is not possible, the box is too full.

Label each box as it is filled. Label only in PENCIL! Labeling should consist of the following: the owning office symbol plus fiscal year in the upper left hand corner label area and the sequential number in the upper right hand corner. Number sequentially, e.g., 1/12, 2/12, etc. If it is unknown how many boxes there will be, just enter the sequence number, then add the whole number to all boxes after completion of the packing job, e.g., 1/ , 2/ , 3/ , 4/ , then go back and add in the total box count at the end: 1/4, 2/4, 3/4, 4/4. The office may contact the museum staff for assigning a unique accession number prior to ascertaining boxes are fully identifiable, especially if multiple groupings of records, or series, will be retired at the same time. Each series group will be assigned a unique number by the museum staff for control purposes and to facilitate later destruction or other action. A fully labeled box may resemble this example:

ACP-99-2   BPA Records   Box ½

This example identifies the second group of records (the "2" is assigned by the Records Center) retired from the Contracting & Procurement Office in Fiscal Year 99, which consists of BPA Records and is the first of two boxes in this grouping to be prepared and retired to the Records Center.

For security, as well as neatness, do not identify the contents of the box on the outside, beyond the simple title shown in the example above. The detailed contents will be outlined in the inventory document.

When packing records, do not stack boxes over four high, any higher tends to begin crushing the boxes. A stack of four boxes can easily be loaded on a hand truck for transport without additional handling.

Preparing Records Inventory or Transfer List

Prepare a records transfer document consisting of a general list of the contents and boxes. A detailed listing of folders is not needed because this information will be entered into the master database at the park museum. If everything is well labeled, this database input can occur very quickly at the museum, and a printed copy of the inventory will be returned to the office for incorporation into the Department's Inactive Records Binder. This is a good chance to double-check to ensure that adequate and consistent labeling has been applied to ALL folders in the box. The general listing may provide the name of the records series, the date range of the records, the number of boxes in the group to be retired, and disposition information if known, also any information that may assist the museum staff in preparing or managing the files during their retirement period.

Where there are multiple folders of a single records title and date range, they will be listed in the database inventory as a group as shown below rather than individually for space and time efficiency. Please ensure that related groupings are appropriately marked with sequential folder numbers, e.g. 1/3, 2/3, 3/3. The inventory listing will appear as:

"BPA File - Ace Hardware - 3 folders

Some types of documents have their own unique number sequences, such as contract files, purchase order files, and time and attendance files by pay period. These types of documents may continue to be in folders as they were in the department (e.g., accordion folders containing all time sheets for a single pay period, etc.). The complete number range of such documents should be correctly listed on the folders, so when the folder headings are used to create the inventory, the information is complete and correct. When preparing the inventory, list the documents in their normal numbering sequence. Consult with records management staff for assistance.

Transferring Prepared Records to the Park Museum

After all above steps have been completed, contact the curator to request physical transfer of the records. The curator or a member of the records staff will come to review the preparations and physically transfer the records to the park museum.

The records always should be physically transferred by museum staff, to protect against damage or loss to the records or personal injury during moving.

An appointment will be scheduled to complete the physical transfer to the park museum. Depending on the current demand, pick-ups may be delayed because of other records intake actions in progress which may be occupying the limited workspace. Records will be picked up as quickly as possible. PLEASE do not move the records to a dangerous storage environment while waiting for pick-up! This includes any basement or unheated building in the park.

After-Transfer Actions

Museum staff will review records boxes and transfer documentation, and make any necessary corrections. Museum staff will perform database entry of the individual file folders in the records accession. Finalized copies of the inventories and transfer forms will be placed on file in the park museum with a tickler system for later action on the records. The staff will send a printout of the completed inventory back to the office, along with a revised Table of Contents for the Department Inactive Records Binder including the newly accessioned and processed material. Please follow the instructions with the inventory and in the Records Binder to incorporate this new material into your department's binder.

Records that are retired by park offices to the park museum remain the property of the office. They will not be available for research to anyone except that office's personnel without the express written permission of the office head.

Records that need to be recalled by the office should be referred to by the accession number, the box number, and the folder title as listed on the records inventory in your department's Inactive Records Binder.

Office staff may request the return of records for a period of 30 days, renewable, or a photocopy of the records. This is to ensure that retrieved records do not become lost and unavailable for further review as needed. One office employee must sign for the records to ensure accountability during the time they are removed from storage.

As scheduled review dates for the records come up, the museum staff will communicate with the owning office regarding the ongoing value of the records for government business. Reviews should occur approximately every two years. These reviews form the basis for further records actions which are normal in the life cycle of records. Many financial and human resources records may be destroyed within a certain period of years. The Records Action Form will initiate further actions, such as a decision to retain records in the park museum for additional time, for destruction, or for transfer of permanently valuable records to the park's archives.

Figure 6 Historic archeology artifacts in storage

Problem Statement

A number of park collections seem to be burdened with materials that probably never should have been retained in the first place. This has been partly the result of too liberal collecting protocols on the part of the archeologist, and partly the park museum collections being used as the park "attic". Examples include 5-gallon cans of coal clinkers from the blacksmith shop excavation at Fort Vancouver; large soil samples from the British Camp excavations at San Juan Island; trash from shovel pit samples at Olympic; and shards of purple bottle glass turned in by visitors at Death Valley (NB: All of this material is currently cataloged, but the validity of the decision to keep any or all of these items is being questioned by the park curators involved.)

Background

According to the FY 2002 Collection Management Report (CMR), the park museum collections in the Pacific West Region contain over 19 million individual items. Approximately 24% are archeological objects and specimens recovered from park lands. Most of these materials resulted from organized excavations or compliance mitigation. A lesser number come from isolated finds made by park staff and visitors. Archeological mitigation continues to occur in almost every park, every year, resulting in thousands of items entering park collections on a continuing basis.

The museum documentation process (accession and catalog) and preparation for storage (basic cleaning, preservation and storage furniture) costs about $100.00 per catalog number assigned. This includes such costs as providing cabinets, shelves and boxes, but does not include building construction or modification for collections work. Storage costs across the region range between $50.00 and $75.00 per cubic foot per year. These costs include such things as heating/air conditioning, annual inventory, conservation/preservation evaluation and application, pest management, emergency operations planning and application, selection and preparation of items for exhibit, making items available for research, and other professional and technical collection management activities. These costs have been well documented in recent years on both regional and national levels. (Bush, 1995; Bohnert, et al, 1997; Child, et al, 2000).

It is obvious that required archeological activities will continue, and will generate materials necessary to document park resources and activities impacting them. These collections and their associated archives also will continue to require documentation, preservation, storage, and management from park collection managers. We have come to the point, however, where we need to be looking closely at what has been retained in the past, and what we want to retain in the future, particularly in light of the costs documented above.

Suggested Actions

There are three actions suggested to rectify this continuing situation at the parks, and to ensure that funds for collections documentation and management are wisely spent:

- Park staffs and archeological and museum professionals in the central offices should review the collecting protocols outlined in park Scope of Collection Statements (SOCS). SOCS should be revised to established appropriate collecting levels for archeological collections.

- Develop suggested general collecting protocol and requirement that some form of this be modified and used for every archeological venture. In this way collecting protocols could be specifically tailored for individual projects as necessary, or the generic protocol could be used. In either case, a copy of the collecting protocol to be used would be discussed with the park collections manager, and included as part of the project record. The project archeologist would also be required to provide the collections manager with a valid description of each item/sample retained, to include the rationale for retention. This information would be entered into the catalog as part of the permanent record, resulting in more complete information in the catalog, as well as documentation as to why the project archeologist felt it important to retain any given item/sample. Currently the protocol and rationale is missing from most documentation, leading to questions and speculation on the part of park curators and managers alike.

- During the cataloging process for currently uncataloged materials (about 26% of the total archeological collections reported in the FY 2002 CMR), archeologists will review items to be cataloged with the curator to determine which items currently accessioned actually need to be cataloged or whether they can be recorded as part of the report and disposed of appropriately.

- The final action is more complex and will take extended cooperation between archeologists and curators over several years. The archeological collections at many parks need to be reviewed by a curator and archeologist team to determine whether the archeological collections at any given park could be improved and made more efficient by judicial de-accessioning activities. This "bi-partisan" review would look at materials such as the Fort Vancouver clinkers, the broken glass at Death Valley, and large soil samples at San Juan Island, to determine whether the disposal of some materials or reduction in the size of some samples, might improve both collections quality and efficiency.

The underpinning philosophy and paradigm of records management within the National Park Service is being rethought in light of NPS best practices and continuing technological impacts on communications. The Department of the Interior (DOI) and the park service have identified the need for continuing management of park cultural and natural resources in two concepts: "Mission Critical Records," as presented in Director's Order #19 (DO#19) and "Resource Management Records," as presented in the DOI and NPS Museum Management policies.

DO#19 specifically identifies mission critical records as having the highest priority in records management activities. Mission critical records are all records documenting natural and cultural resources and their previous management. These records contain information crucial for the future management of the resources and include "…general management plans and other major planning documents that record basic management, and philosophies and policies, or that direct park management and activities for long periods of time."

Other examples of mission critical records include records that directly support the specific mission of a park unit and the overall mission of the park service. These records are permanent records that will eventually become archival records. Therefore, DO#19 dictates that these records should receive archival care as soon as practical in their life cycle.

Similar to mission critical records is the concept of resource management records. The DOI manual defines resource management records as "made or acquired by the federal government to record information on cultural and natural resources." As described in the *Cultural Resources Management Guideline* (DO#28), resource management records document park resources and provide key information for their continuing management. Accordingly, they are classified as "library and museum materials made or acquired and preserved solely for reference or exhibition purposes." Therefore, these materials are excluded from the National Archives' definition of records.

However, in the last few years the definition of resource management records has broadened beyond reference or exhibition materials. Many official records have also been designated as important for the long-term management of park cultural and natural resources. In the past, official records could not be added to a park's museum or library collection. However, records generated by the planning process and compliance review actions of resource management are important official records that never reach an inactive status.

The past system of records management and disposition as promulgated in NPS-19 focused on "official records" and "unofficial records." Official records were original documents created or received by a park in the course of performing the daily business of the NPS. Unofficial, or sub-official, records encompassed duplicate copies of official records and documents generated in association with a resource management project (e.g., archeological field notes).

Non-official records were materials not created by a government agency, and included donated manuscripts (e.g., letters written by an eminent figure associated with the creation of a park), collections of personal papers, organizational records of non-governmental entities such as businesses or civic groups, and collections accrued by private individuals.

Only sub-official and non-official records could be placed in a park's museum collection, after evaluation against the park's Scope of Collection Statement (SOCS) for retention if appropriate. By law NARA has been responsible for the official records of the federal government, once the records are no longer actively needed and have reached their disposition date. Non-official records, such as manuscript collections, were not governed by the NPS Records Disposition Schedule and NARA and included in a park's museum collection based upon its SOCS.

Under the new methodology, instead of a record's importance being primarily dictated by its form (a signed original or a copy), it is now to be determined by the actual information it carries. This philosophy divides records into "permanent" and "temporary;" copies are to be considered just copies and so are not addressed. Permanent records have continuing value to resource management. Temporary records have a limited use life in the operations of a park (or support office). Permanently active records are also discussed; these are materials needed for the long-term, ongoing management of park resources for the NPS to fulfill its agency mandate.

The criteria for permanent and temporary also take into account the office of creation—a permanent record for one office, such as a regional office, may be temporary for a park because it is a distributed copy for general reference only. Temporary records are to be retained as long as indicated by the revised Records Retention Schedule. After their allotted retention time, temporary records may be disposed of by parks or retained longer if still needed.

Many of the disposition time frames outlined in NPS-19 have been retained in the new DO#19 retention schedule. This applies in particular to fiscal, routine administrative, law enforcement, forms covered under NARA General Records Schedule 20, and other daily operational materials. Permanent records may also be retained as long as actively needed for use and reference. Under the new DO#19, permanent records are to include land acquisition records, park planning documents, documents pertaining to cultural and resource management decisions and projects, and documents pertaining to the history of the administration and interpretation of a park.

The concept of resource management records has been broadened in DO#19 from definitions in NPS-19 that classified only associated project records as permanent, such as archeological field notes and natural history project data. Currently, the park service Records Advisory Council (RAC) has suspended disposition of certain official records that may be important for parks to retain on-site. The new, broadened concept classifies as permanent a wide array of documents previously considered temporary (such as construction reports) because the subject of the document is a park resource or substantially impacts a park resource. For example, previously all contracts were considered temporary, whereas the broadened definition of resource management records considers contracts on cultural resources (e.g., a historic building on the National Register of Historic Places) permanent.

Under the new NARA protocol, parks will have three avenues to choose among to provide accessibility to their inactive (no longer actively needed or in use) records before the records are permanently destroyed or retired to the National Archives. Under the new proposal, parks may still send inactive records to a NARA FRC for public access and storage following the current procedure, but now a fee will be charged by the Office of Management and Budget ($3.28 per cubic foot as of Oct. 2000). This charge is currently being paid by WASO for all parks.

Parks can now arrange for storage at an off-site commercial repository, or retain their own records on-site. In both cases, professional archival parameters of preservation and access set by NARA must be met. These archival parameters include security, fire protection, appropriate storage techniques, climate controlled environment, and widely disseminated collection finding aids. Most if not all of these parameters are met at the NOCA curatorial storage area at Marblemount. Once the inactive records have reached their disposition date, records are to be destroyed or transferred to the National Archives for permanent storage. These new changes in records definitions and storage procedures will not be reflected in DO#28 *Cultural Resources Management Guideline* and the *NPS Museum Handbook*, Part II, Appendix D, "Museum Archives and Manuscript Collections," until these documents are revised.

Records managers recommend parks establish comprehensive, stand-alone project files for resource management, major special events, park infrastructure and research projects, and that these project files not be assigned NPS file codes (see Appendix A, page 85). These files should contain copies of finalized contract documents including substantive change orders and specifications, requisition forms, "as-built" documents for finished construction projects, related project planning documents and all documents illustrating all decisions made and why. For research projects, project files should also include copies of all researcher field notes, laboratory notes and results, a copy of the final report and report drafts, and any other materials generated by the project in question. Staff are then assured that a full set of documents covering an entire project are gathered, in order of creation and project evolution, in one place. It also averts problems of fiscal records being filed separately from other project materials, and potentially losing critical data from a project's life history.

When a project is completed, its files should be retired to the park's museum archives for long-term reference. The separation of routine administrative records from project records is recommended practice in the General Records Schedules as well. NARA expects that routine administrative records are temporary with short retention spans before destruction. Project records, on the other hand, are expected to have long retention periods, be permanent, and have potential (if not anticipated) archival value.

The *NPS Museum Handbook,* Part II, Appendix D, "Museum Archives and Manuscript Collections," governing the creation and management of park archives and manuscript collections, does not reflect this paradigm shift. It reflects the guidelines of NPS-19, and states that non-official records, or only "associated project records," are eligible to be retained by a park for its museum collection archives. The new paradigm is also not reflected in DO#28, *Cultural Resources Management Guideline.* Both Appendix D and DO#28 will be revised to reflect the changes in NARA policy and NPS records management upon their finalization.

Good museum management planning requires an understanding of the library, archives, and museum collection resources as they currently exist; background on how and why these resources were developed; and information on what is required to preserve the resources and make them available for use. In order to accomplish these goals effectively, planners must first review park-specific documentation such as reports, checklists, and plans, then make recommendations based on professional theory and techniques that are documented in the professional literature.

This bibliography provides the references used in developing this *Museum Management Plan*. The first section gives references to park-specific documentation used by the team to understand the current status of the resources. The second section includes a list of recommended readings that will provide park staff with a better understanding of the physical and intellectual nature of these unique resources, and will enable them to apply professionally accepted techniques and standards for preservation and use.

Park Reference List

Bush, K., et al. *Collection Management Plan: North Cascades National Park*, 1994.

Florence. *North Cascades National Park Service Complex Historic Structures Preservation Guide*, North Cascades National Park Service Complex 1987.

Gilbert and Luxenberg. *Cultural Landscape Inventory of the Buckner Orchard,* North Cascades National Park Service Complex, 1984.

Kennedy, J. *Buckner Homestead Historic District Final Management Plan*. North Cascades National Park Service Complex, 1998.

Louter, David. *Contested Terrain: An Administrative History.* North Cascades National Park Service Complex, 1998.

Luxenberg, Gretchen A. *Historic Resource Study.* North Cascades National Park Service Complex, 1986.

Luxenberg, Gretchen A. *Historic Structures Inventory.* North Cascades National Park Service Complex, 1984.

McKinley, Laura. 1993. *An Unbroken Historical Record: An Administrative History Of Ebey's Landing National Historical Reserve.* National Park Service.

National Park Service. *General Management Plan for North Cascades National Park; Ross Lake National Recreation Area and Lake Chelan National Recreation Area.* U.S. Government Printing Office 1988-573-038/60,031 Region No. 8, July 1988.

_____. *Interpretive Prospectus: North Cascades National Park, Ross Lake National Recreation Area, Lake Chelan National Recreation Area, Washington,* 1990.

_____. *Lake Chelan National Recreation Area General Management Plan,* 1995.

_____. *List of Classified Structures.* 2004. The List of Classified Structures (LCS) is an evaluated inventory of all historic and prehistoric structures that have historical, architectural, and/or engineering significance within parks of the National Park System.

_____. *Long-Term Ecological Monitoring Conceptual Plan.* North Cascades National Park Service Complex, June 2004.

_____. *Strategic Plan for North Cascades National Park Service Complex: Fiscal Year 2001 – 2005 (October 1, 2000 - September 30, 2005).* North Cascades National Park Service Complex, 2000.

Trust Board of Ebey's Landing National Historical Reserve. *Mission Statement.* 1994.

_____. *Vision Statement.* 1994.

U.S. Congress. An Act to establish the North Cascades National Park and Ross Lake and Lake Chelan National Recreation Areas, to designate the Pasayten Wilderness and to modify the Glacier Peak Wilderness, in the State of Washington, and for other purposes. (82 Stat. 926) October 2, 1968.

_____. An Act to designate wilderness within Olympic National Park, Mount Rainier National Park, and North Cascades National Park Service Complex in the State of Washington, and for other purposes. (102 Stat. 3961) November 16, 1988.

_____. An Act to preserve and protect a rural community which provides an unbroken historical record from nineteenth century exploration and settlement in Puget Sound to the present time. Ebey's Landing National Historical Reserve, (92 Stat. 3508) November 10, 1978 .

Suggested Reading List

The skills and craft necessary to perform adequate curatorial work have expanded exponentially over the past three decades. Fortunately, the literature in the field has also expanded to meet program needs. The current National Park Service publications, *NPS Museum Handbook*, the *Conserve O Gram* series, and *Tools of the Trade,* all provide basic guidelines. They inform the reader how to perform certain tasks such as accessioning and cataloging, but they do not teach the neophyte when and/or why these tasks should be done. The proper application of the methodology presented in these documents requires a degree of intellectual preparation and practical experience that cannot be provided in procedural manuals or a two-week course.

The following references represent some of the best theory and practice in the fields of collection management, exhibits and programs, and archival management available today within the professional community. The museum management planning team does not suggest that the park purchase a copy of each suggested reference, but it is possible to acquire copies of these volumes on inter-library loan.

Park managers and supervisors are encouraged to consider familiarity with the recognized literature in the field when evaluating prospective employees or, as an indication of continued professional growth when doing performance evaluations. This familiarity should be a determining factor for employment at the GS 1015/11 level and above. It should also serve as an indication of job interest and commitment to professionalism when overall work standards are evaluated.

Collection Management References

American Association of Museums. *Caring for Collections: Strategies for Conservation, Maintenance and Documentation*. 1984. More than 60 curators, registrars, and conservators contributed information on how to improve environmental conditions, manage inventory, register objects, and augment public use of museum collections.

Appelbaum, Barbara. *Guide to Environmental Protection of Collections*. Second View Press, 1991. Clarifies the various conditions that impact collections, how objects respond, and how to mitigate damage. Good book for the non-specialist.

Butcher-Younghans, Sherry. *Historic House Museums: A Practical Handbook for Their Care, Preservation, and Management*. Oxford University Press, 1996. This book serves as both reference and hands-on guide for all aspects of historic house management, including collections care, conservation, security, and interpretation.

Buck, Rebecca A. & Gilmore, Jean A., eds. *The New Museum Registration Methods*. American Association of Museums, 1998. This is a very well done update of the classic *Museum Registration Methods* by Dorothy Dudley and Irma Wilkinson (below). Good format and easy to reference, with up-to-date information sections concerning copyright, NAGPRA issues, and ethics.

Committee on Libraries, Museums, and Historic Buildings. *Protection of Museums and Museum Collections 1980*. NFPA 911, Boston: National Fire Protection Association, Inc., 1980. One of the best sources on fire protection and prevention, written specifically for museums.

Dudley, Dorothy H., et al. *Museum Registration Methods.* 3rd ed. American Association of Museums, 1979. Accepted as "the basic reference" for museum registrars, this classic covers registration, storage, and care, as well as insurance, packing and shipping, and loan management.

Edwards, Stephen R., Bruce M. Bell, and Mary Elizabeth King. *Pest Control in Museums: A Status Report*. Lawrence, Kansas: Association of Systematic Collections, 1980. A good guide to pesticides, their use in museums, and common insect pests.

Hensley, John R. "Safeguarding Museum Collections from the Effects of Earthquakes." *Curator*, September 1987, pp. 199-205.

Hunter, John E. "Standard Practices for Handling Museum Objects." Omaha, Nebraska: National Park Service, Midwest Region. North Dakota.

_____. "Standards for the Design, Installation, Testing, and Maintenance of Interior Intrusion Detection/Alarm System." Omaha, Nebraska: National Park Service, Midwest Region. 1981.

Johnson, E. Verner and Joanne C. Horgan. *Museum Collection Storage*. Paris: UNESCO, 1979.

Knell, Susan. *Care of Collections*. London: Routledge, 1994. Basic book on preventative conservation, focusing on specific and practical guidelines for collections care and handling.

Leo, Jack. "How to Secure Your Museum: A Basic Checklist." *History News*, June 1980, pp. 10-12.

Lewis, Ralph H. *Manual for Museums*. Washington, DC: National Park Service, Department of Interior, 1976.

MacLeish, A. Bruce. *The Care of Antiques and Historical Collections*. Nashville, Tennessee: The American Association for State and Local History, 1983. A reference for general museum collection care.

Malaro, M.C., *A Legal Primer on Managing Museum Collections*. Washington, DC: Smithsonian Institutional Press, 1985.

Metsger, Deborah A. & Shelia C. Byers, eds. *Managing the Modern Herbarium: An Interdisciplinary Approach*. 1999. Society for the Preservation of Natural History Collections. Elton-Wolfe Publishing, Vancouver, Canada. First significant publication in decades on herbaria that covers all aspects of herbaria management.

National Park Service. *Automated National Catalog System User Manual*. 1998.

_____.*Conserve O Gram*. 1974 to present.

_____.*CRM*, Volume 22, no. 2, 1999 "Archives at the Millennium."

_____.NPS *Management Policies*. 2001.

_____.*NPS Museum Handbook*, Part I: Museum Collections. 1990 (revised).

_____.*NPS Museum Handbook*, Part II: Museum Records. 2000.

_____. *NPS Museum Handbook*, Part III: Museum Collections Use. 1998.

_____. DO#19: *Records Management*. 2001.

_____. NPS-19: *Records Management Guidebook*. 1999 Appendix B (only): "Records Management Disposition Schedule."

_____. DO#28: *Cultural Resources Management Guideline*. 1998.

_____. NPS-77: *Natural Resources Management Guideline*. 1991.

_____. DO#24: NPS *Museum Collection Management*, 2000.

_____. *Tools of the Trade*. 1996.

Reitherman, Robert. "Protection of Museum Contents from Earthquakes." The J. Paul Getty Museum Symposium on Protection of Art Objects from Damage by Earthquakes: What Can Be Done? 1984.

Rose, Carolyn and Amparo de Torres, eds. *Storage of Natural History Collections: Ideas and Practical Solutions.* Society for the Preservation of Natural History Collections, 1992. A good "idea" book containing several photographs and graphics detailing innovative solutions to the storage of various types of materials.

_____ & C.A. Hawks, et al. *Storage of Natural History Collections: A Preventive Conservation Approach.* 1995. Society for the Preservation of Natural History Collections.

Thomson, Garry. *The Museum Environment.* 2nd ed. London: Butterworths, 1986. An excellent source on light, humidity, and air pollution.

Thomson, John, et al. *Manual of Curatorship: A Guide to Museum Practice.* 2nd ed. London: Butterworths, 1992. Possibly the best comprehensive reference in print on the craft and professionalism required for curatorial work.

Weinstein, Robert A., et al. *Collection, Use and Care of Historical Photographs.* American Association for State and Local History, 1977. One of the best basic references on this technical subject.

Zycherman, Linda, ed. *A Guide to Museum Pest Control.* The Foundation of the American Institute for Conservation of Historic and Artistic Works, and the Association of Systematic Collections. A good, basic reference on pest identification, with suggestions for methods of control.

References for Exhibits and Programs

American Association of Museums. "The Audience in Exhibition Development: Course Proceedings." *Resource Report*, 1992. A good guide to models of exhibition development; philosophy of education; learning theory; gender, culture, class and learning; spatial knowledge and its role in learning; evaluation; and visitor surveys.

Belcher, Michael. *Exhibitions in Museums*. Smithsonian Institution Press, 1992. Discusses every stage of exhibit planning, design, and presentation, including audience research and evaluation. A good resource book.

Dean, David. *Museum Exhibition: Theory and Practice*. London: Routledge, 1994. Outlines the full range of exhibition development concerns, from planning and design to evaluation and administration.

Falk, John and Lynn D. Dierking. *The Museum Experience*. Whalesback Books, 1992. Provides a good introduction to what is known about why people go to museums, what they do there, and what they learn. Guidelines and recommendations are offered to help museum staff understand visitors and their motivation for visiting.

Hooper-Greenhill, Eileen. *Museums and Their Visitors*. London: Routledge, 1994. The unique needs of school groups, families, and people with disabilities are outlined and illustrated with examples of exhibit, education, and marketing policies that work to provide a quality visitor experience.

Hooper-Greenhill, Eileen, ed. *The Educational Role of the Museum*. London: Routledge, 1994. A close look at the theories of communication in museums, exhibition theories and case studies, and educational programs in British museums, this book translates well into the American experience.

Korn, Randi and Laurie Sowd. *Visitor Surveys: A User's Manual*. American Association of Museums, 1990. A good, basic manual on how to conduct visitor surveys to accurately measure the effectiveness of museum exhibits and programs.

McLean, Kathleen. *Planning for People in Museum Exhibitions*. Association of Science-Technology Centers, 1993. Good description of the exhibition process, from planning to assessment.

New York Hall of Science. *Take to the Streets: Guide to Planning Outdoor, Public Exhibits.* 1995. Based on a series of sidewalk exhibits done in New York, this book contains checklists and guidelines for planning, designing, and implementing outdoor exhibits.

Neil, Arminta. *Help for the Small Museum.* Pruett Publishing Co. 1987. The second edition of the classic "how to" book for the development of temporary exhibits on a tight budget.

Serrell, Beverly. *Exhibit Labels: An Interpretive Approach.* Altamira Press, 1996. Solid reference tool, including discussions of label planning, writing, design, and publication. Contains very good resource list, glossary, and bibliography.

Witteborg, Lothar P. *Good Show! A Practical Guide for Temporary Exhibitions.* Smithsonian Institution Traveling Exhibition Service, 1991. The second edition of a standard reference offering practical guidance in exhibit planning, design, fabrication, security, conservation, and installation.

Archives Management References

Adela, James M. *Understanding Archives and Manuscripts.* Archival Fundamentals Series, Chicago: Society of American Archivists, 1990.

Aourada, Stephen. *Archives and Manuscript Materials in Parks of the North Atlantic Region.* National Park Service, 1992.

Association of British Archivists, Small Archives Committee. *A Manual for Small Archives,* British Columbia: Association of British Columbia Archivists, 1988.

Baird, Donald and Laura M. Coles. *A Manual for Small Archives.* Vancouver: Archives Association of British Columbia, 1991.

Bellardo, Lewis and Lynn Lady Bellardo. *A Glossary for Archivists, Manuscript Curators, and Records Managers.* Archival Fundamental Series. Chicago: Society of American Archivists, 1992.

Casterline, Gail F. *Archives and Manuscripts: Exhibits*. Chicago: Society of American Archivists, 1980 (Out-of-print).

Cook, Michael. Archives Administration: *A Manual for Intermediate and Small Organizations and for Local Government*. Folkestone, England: William Dawson and Sons, 1977.

Cox, Richard J. *Managing Institutional Archives*. New York: Greenwood Press, 1982.

Daniels, Maygene and Timothy Walsh, eds. *A Modern Archives Reader: Basic Readings on Archival Theory and Practice.* Washington, DC: National Archives Trust Fund Board, 1984.

Eastman-Kodak. *Conservation of Photographs*. Rochester, NY: Kodak publication F-40, Rochester, NY: Eastman-Kodak Company, 1985.

Ellis, Judith, ed. *Keeping Archives*. Second edition. Australia: Australian Society of Archivists and D.W. Thorpe, 1993.

Finch, Elsie Freeman, ed. *Advocating Archives: An Introduction to Public Relations for Archivists*. Chicago: Society of American Archivists, 1994.

Ham, Gerald F. *Selecting and Appraising Archives and Manuscripts*. Archival Fundamental Series. Chicago: Society of American Archivists, 1992.

Harrison, Donald Fisher, ed. *Automation in Archives*. Washington, DC: Mid-Atlantic Regional Archives Conference, 1993.

Hensen, Steven. *Archives, Personal Papers, and Manuscripts: A Cataloging Manual for Archival Repositories, Historical Societies, and Manuscript Libraries.* 2nd ed., Chicago: Society of American Archivists, 1990. http://www.archivists.org

Hunter, Greg. *Developing and Maintaining Practical Archives*. New York: Neal Schuman Publishers, 1997.

Kesner, Richard and Lisa Weber. *Automating the Archives: A Beginner's Guide*. Chicago: Society of American Archivists, 1991.

Miller, Frederic M. *Arranging and Describing Archives and Manuscripts*. Archival Fundamental Series. Chicago: Society of American Archivists, 1990.

National Archives and Records Administration (NARA). *A NARA Evaluation: The Management of Audiovisual Records in Federal Agencies. A General Report.* Washington, DC, 1991.

MacNeil, Heather. *Without Consent: The Ethics of Disclosing Personal Information in Public Archives.* Metuchen, New Jersey: Scarecrow Press, 1992.

O'Toole, James M. *Understanding Archives and Manuscripts*. Archival Fundamental Series. Chicago: Society of American Archivists, 1990.

Pugh, Mary Jo. *Providing Reference Services for Archives and Manuscripts*. Archival Fundamental Series. Chicago: Society of American Archivists, 1992.

Ritzenthaler, Mary Lynn, et al. *Archives and Manuscripts: Administration of Photographic Collections*. SAA Basic Manual Series. Chicago: Society of American Archivists, 1984.

Ritzenthaler, Mary Lynn. *Preserving Archives and Manuscripts*. Archival Fundamental Series. Chicago: Society of American Archivists, 1993.

Rogers, Paul. "Evaluation of Records Management and Archives Administration in the National Park Service" (MA Thesis, Western Washington University, 2003).

Silverman, Cetyl and Nancy J. Perezo. *Preserving the Anthropological Record.* New York: Wanner-Green Foundation for Anthropological Research, Inc., 1992.

Swartzburg, Susan. *Preserving Library Materials*: A Manual. 2nd ed. Metuchen, NJ: Scarecrow Press, 1995.

Van Bogart, Dr. John W.C. *Magnetic Tape Storage and Handling: A Guide for Libraries and Archives*. Washington, DC: The Commission on Preservation and Access, 1995.

Warren, Susan. "Introduction to Archival Organization and Description: Access to Cultural Heritage." Getty Information Institute: San Marino, CA, 1998. On-the-Web primer includes a tutorial at http://www.schistory.org/getty/index.html

Wilted, Thomas and William Note. *Managing Archival and Manuscript Repositories*. Archival Fundamental Series. Chicago: Society of American Archivists, 1991.

Yakel, Elizabeth. *Starting an Archives*. Chicago: Society of American Archivists, 1994.

www.ingramcontent.com/pod-product-compliance
Lightning Source LLC
Chambersburg PA
CBHW081133170526
45165CB00008B/2660